Flipping The Scripts:

How To Reject Society's Narratives and Write Your Own Destiny

Academic Edition

Alan Gaines

Copyright © 2018 by Alan Gaines

All rights reserved. No part of this book may be reproduced by any mechanical, photographic, or electronic process, or in the form of a phonographic recording: nor may it be stored in a retrieval systems, transmitted, or otherwise be copied for public or private use - other than for "fair use" as brief quotations embodied in articles and reviews - without prior permission of the author.

For more information:

rejectingthenarrative@gmail.com

Order this book at:
http://www.flippingthescripts.com

Cover design by: DeShawn Noblesse
Edited & Proofread by: Safi Banks

ISBN 978-0-692-06251-7

To My Wife, Carla
Words Can't Express What You Mean To Me and How You Support Everything That I Do, So Let Me Just Say That I Am Fortunate and Your Love Is Evidence That God Loves Me...

Dedicated to Ernest Stansil…
The True Definition of A Man - God knew that I needed guidance and direction on the road to Manhood and he put you in my life from the very 1st Day that I was Born. I always hated the title "StepFather" but in Hindsight it is Appropriate because you carefully guided my Steps and gave me the knowledge that I am passing on in this Book.

To My Brothers Sherray & EJ And My Uncle Trey
Ray For Teaching Me How To Be "That Guy" & EJ For Holding Me Accountable. Uncle Trey For Always Putting A Positive Path For Me to Follow

For My Only Son
Hannibal Chockwe Akinwole Uhuru
Hopefully, These Lessons Will Allow You To Lead The Life That I Did Not Know How
To Lead Until I Was In My 30's…

In Memory of Kalief Browder -
Your Life Defined A Rejection of the Narrative
May Your Legacy Inspire Generations For All Eternity

Special Thanks To
Allen Iverson
Your Relentless Approach To The Game And Unwillingness To Conform And Apologize For Who And What You Are Off The Court Is The Spirit That This Book Is Written With… I Tried To Mimic You On The Court and Now I Write With That Same Passion and Conviction

Special Thanks to Safi Banks -
Couldn't Have Done This Without You!!! Thanks for Your Knowledge, Feedback and Editorial Advice

Table of Contents

Foreword: For The Parents by Alan Gaines & Michael G. Thomas Jr. V

Introduction: For The Young Males of The World VI

Chapter 1: What is the Narrative? 3

Chapter 2: Who Gives Us The Narrative 19

Chapter 3: Going To College and Getting A Job Makes You Successful 27

Chapter 4: If My Daddy Was Here, Everything Would Be Alright With Me........ 41

Chapter 5: Everybody Else Is Doing It 53

Chapter 6: Social Media is Killing Your Potential 61

Chapter 7: Being A Gangster / Thug Is Cool 71

Chapter 8: How Many Bodies You Got? The Narrative & Womanizing 85

Chapter 9: Nobody Makes It From Here 97

Chapter 10: Smoking Or Drinking Will Solve Your Problems 105

Chapter 11: It Was How I Was Raised / The Taboo 113

Chapter 12: Write Your Own Destiny 127

Appendix I: A Message To The Parents 139

Appendix II: A Message To Young Males of the World 140

Acknowledgements 141

About The Author 144

Foreword: For The Parents

Please, if you will, read this with your child, read this to your child, feel free to share your stories and experiences to help articulate these points even further. Let this book serve as a discussion starter or a frame of reference when trying to lead your child out of the trap house of mediocrity that leads to a life of depression and unfulfilled potential.

I don't intend to be an expert, nor do I feel that my opinion is the end all be all or the only way in which you can make progress. I am fully aware that what we face in the hood is not going to be solved with the words within this book.

However, I will commit to being open, honest and revealing in hopes of allowing young males to look at themselves and to reflect on the situations around them. My hope is that our sons will find the strength to live the life that they choose because they feel confident and empowered to be who God made them to be and who they truly want to show the world.

It is my sincerest hope that this book, allows you and your son to have a very open and honest conversation about the things that he is facing as he navigates through this world full of pitfalls and trappings.So as you read or if you allow them to read it alone, please encourage them to remain positive and to work hard at their gifts because it will be the cultivating of these gifts that will bring them everything they deserve in life. This Quote from one of the early readers of the book perfectly conveys the essence of the book...

"If you are struggling with having life conversations with the young men in your life because it's uncomfortable, you don't feel it's your place, or you don't feel you can relate, this book will help you find common ground in those conversations.This is my recommended summer reading for fathers and sons, uncles and nephews, coaches and players, etc. Lastly, this book isn't just about faulty narratives. It is also a challenge to men to create safe spaces, support and resources to young men whose passions and desires are not being adequately nurtured." Alan Gaines, thank you for not allowing the narratives of old prevent you from executing your vision.

- Michael G. Thomas Jr.

Accredited Financial Counselor / Ph.D Candidate

Introduction: For The Young Males of The World

The goal of this book is to allow you to find the strength inside yourself to create the world and life that you want and stop accepting the life that you have been "told" rather directly or indirectly you should lead. I want you to embrace who you are. To no longer be embarrassed of your talents and gifts that others may find silly or you feel will be made fun of. Too often we as Black males and men, abandon our dreams and talents because of how we feel our peers will look at us. We put our talents down and in a lot of cases we never pick them up again.

Growing up, I accepted many narratives and did many things that were unbecoming of the person I wanted to be and who I truly am deep down. However, I, like many of you, felt that I had an image to uphold and a reputation to maintain, so I did what I felt I had to do to support and protect that persona. Which, as you will see throughout this book took me away from my childhood goals.

So let's begin this journey of self and society reflection and take a long look at the role we are playing. We will compare and contrast it to the person we are when we are alone in the room with just our thoughts and no one else is there to judge us.

I want you to know that before we go any further, I am giving you this because I have an undying love for you and that I know that what you hold inside can and will change the world and generations to come. This can only happen when you finally embrace who you are and stop apologizing for and hiding from yourself.

Please feel free… Read on, disagree, take these words and extend them, take these words and reject them if they don't fit. I only ask that you be open… Don't come into this feeling like someone is not listening to you and giving you another preaching about your short comings and the downfalls of your generation… This is a book that will, if you let it, teach you to examine the situation before you move and give you the strength to make that move with no regards to how others will feel if you know in your heart this is the right and moral thing to do…

So, as y'all would say…. LEEEETTTTTTT'SSSSS GOOOOOOOOOO!!!

Understanding The Narrative...

Section 1:

How Life Gives Us The Scripts and Applies Pressure On Us, Insisting That We Play The Roles...

"Physical violence in young males is usually the result of their inability to accurately express their thoughts and emotions. We must challenge both the idea that fighting is a viable solution to our problems as well as violence being a measure of ones strength. True strength is found in the ability to think through situations and finding a solution that brings you closer to your goals or the things you may want out of life."

- Alan Gaines

Chapter 1:
What is the Narrative?

"Bro look at your hairline tho" – "Look at your hairline…" "Boyyyy" – "Yo lining look like Stevie Wonder is yo Barber!" "Yo linin' look like it was done with a spork" "Bro you weak, why are you even talkin' to me?" "Bro, I'm weak? How I'm weak?" "You weak, you don't get no girls, you wear the same outfits every other week and look at your shoes… What are those????" "Bro, I don't got girls? Bro I got more thots than you, who you got?" "I got your mama, nigga now what?" "Bro, watch your mouth before you catch these hands!" "Nigga what you think I am supposed to be scared of you, nigga wsup?" "Shiidd wsup then nigga?" " You a b…."

    And there it is… What started out as joking now has become a test of someone's manhood. Once he called him a "bi#$%" we all knew it was about to be a fight… "I know you can't just let nobody disrespect you like that! I don't care what you talking about, I ain't about to let nobody call me no "B"! – That's probably what you are thinking and saying to yourself as you just read this scenario that we have heard and seen too many times to count. I get it, I am not going to sit here and front and act like I have not been in that situation myself – here is how mine played out in my 8th grade year:

So we were in WoodShop class at Tolleston Middle School – I'm in the back of the class, which is rather big because it has machines that literally cut wood inside of it and is like a mini warehouse almost. So me, my boys CP and A Sain are in the back of the class, we are definitely goofing off and halfway paying attention. So I get to roasting on this kid in the classroom – we never truly got along, he really didn't have no status on the popularity scale and I did so by all accounts I am bullying this kid because I am picking on him and I know for sure he didn't start up with me. I'm just keeping it 💯. I can't write this and act like I was perfect. Ok, so to make a long story short, he gets tired of me going in and he just says "F- You, You Punk A$# Pu#$%".Everyone turns if I was TuPac – You know, All Eyes On Me! Now remember, I just said I have a rank at the school. Everybody know me, I can't let this slide if I wanted to. I got to fight him now because words will not be enough in this situation, he has disrespected my manhood and I had to save face (My thinking at the time, not now. Remember this point because we will talk about it more in a later chapter).
 So yes, we threw hands…

Ok, let's get back to the point which is: 1) I should have never started picking on him – my actions put him in a position in which he felt that he must defend himself – eventually everyone has to confront the bully. 2) Where do we get this idea of manhood and that certain words (like being called a B-) must trigger this attack dog reaction to its space being invaded?

The purpose of this book is to tackle this question and other in a real way that you can relate to. And also help you realize that you have a limitless amount of power within you, which when you tap into it, will help you create a world beyond anything you have imagined so far in your life. I often hear people say, "When you know better, you do better". Well this book is going to help you "know better." I truly feel that the majority of the actions I partook in as a teen and into early adulthood were because I lacked true awareness. That is no one's fault but my own. However, I know too many people who say, "If I knew then, what I know now, things would be so much different." I don't want you to be one of those people that feel this way, so let's dig into this book.

I know that you are like, "Ok this seems cool, but what is The Narrative? What are you talking about?" Gotcha here we go…

The Narrative, as I call it and will refer to it throughout this book, are the behaviors that we have been told both directly and indirectly define our manhood and because we accept and do not question these "thoughts" we feel that we must act them out in order to be a man. These are some very common examples of how we hear the narrative:

1) That girl got you whipped you! You probably telling her you love her!
2) I bet you ain't getting none though…
3) You a nerd bro – why you doing your school work, you a kiss up
4) Stop whining, you soft!
5) Bro, you gone let him disrespect you like that? I know you not gone let that ride! Bro you better handle that…

These are just some of the things we hear growing up and because we think and are told to feel that this is normal, although deep down we know that this is in conflict with our natural emotions. In turn, we deny ourselves and what we feel and conform to what our "friends" or others are telling us is the way we should handle the situation.

This denial of ourselves stems from a lack of self confidence and the natural desire to have love and acceptance. The natural desire to be loved and accepted is something that every individual is born with. I urge you to look up emotional development of humans if you want to get more into why, however, I want to stay on topic, so let's keep going.

When we deny our natural emotions and reactions that we feel and conform to what those around us are telling us we should or better do, we have accepted a Narrative that we genuinely do not agree with. Finding ourselves in these situations does not feel good, because all eyes are on us and we can not escape these defining moments and more often than not, our reactions in that moment are to meet the needs of love and acceptance that our "boys" provide. I get it, no one wants to be an outcast. However, I want you to have the courage to choose your own path and not play the expected role that you have been given by society.

How We Accept the Narrative

These interactions and encounters with The Narrative essentially lead you to contemplating and eventually creating a persona that in some (often many) ways does not reflect who we are inside. This "new you" is designed with armor to protect us from these awkward feelings we get in these encounters/confrontations in which our "manhood" is either in question or being put to the test. Here is an example of what that can look like and all too often is happening in our search to manhood.

Ok, so you finally got that girl that you been feeling, since like the 5th grade. I mean everybody liked her but you got her! If that's not the case you got the girl that you been wanting to get with for the longest of time! Everything is cool, she feeling you, you feeling her… The whole vibe is good, everything is "Gucci". Alright, so, one day you're at your boy crib or your friends are at your spot – y'all all kicking it – playing 2k or Call of Duty and talking bout girls. You got your chest poked out because you got the one you want and your good. Little do you know having her is not enough anymore. One of your boys is telling everybody that him and ole girl starting to fool around. She letting him put his hands in places that mommy said were off limits, even more, she doing things to him that they talk about in the videos! By this time the game is completely paused and everyone is all ears, he spilling the details – its way too detailed to be a made up story… Next thing you know he pulls out his phone and he showing you the text and the pictures she sent… So now everybody like whoaaaa…

Now, let's take a look at this scene from more than just a personal perspective – of course, this type of thing is what you want to do, because you have already seen or been exposed to more than what someone your age should have in regards to sex. So the desire is there and ain't no stopping it. More than just the physical affection that he got, let's look at the response he got from his boys. No other way to put it… HE IS THE MAN!!! – He getting love and respect because he has made it farther with a girl so far than anyone in the room and although it's not a race – hence – the old school word "fast"- you know "she fast" that referenced girls who were promiscuous. Nowadays y'all say "she going" or she is a "Thot". Part of you wants that love and praise that everyone is showering on your boy. But hey, you got ole girl and you put in a lot of work to get her and more importantly – YOU RESPECT HER – you like who she is and that feeling is strong. You truly want to make her happy. You carry her books, you walk with her to class, you legit like this girl and she likes you, she is a good girl and you are proud of that, she even makes you feel good about yourself.

Oh, but the conversation at the house is not over. Boys will be boys as they say, so now… Somebody get's to lyin' – he did this, he did that – he don't want to be left out he conversation, so he just making up stuff – everybody know he lyin' – but he's your boy so its cool. Plus, he don't got much status anyway but he cool peoples and y'all keep him around. So next up is the friend who don't got a girl and ain't had one – he gets clowned for a second but not long – he doesn't like being teased plus he is probably still in that awkward stage and girls aren't really feeling him much so – its all good. Now the conversation swings to you….

They get to roasting you – "Awww he in love"… "She ain't gone let you even get your feel on" "You be carrying her books" "She got you whipped" etc… Your boys are letting you have it and you like ole girl so you stand up for her and yourself and they back off.

Cool, you made it out that one safe, but now in your mind things have changed. Now, your eyes and mind are set on making a move on your girl. Just being her man ain't good enough anymore, you know that you can't endure too many more of those talks with your boys and not have something to add. Plus, you want some physical affection anyway so, it's a win win for you!!! Right??? Well let's pick this back up later, for now we will pause and look at the conversation and more elements of what just took place… – You have just accepted That Narrative and now let's see how you are likely to go play out that script.

Situations like this happen all the time, it's probably happening as we speak in multiple cities across the country. As a young man in training, let's keep it 💯. Mama never told you about this and the guy that you looked up to is usually someone just a tad bit too old or in the wrong position to talk to you about things like this without contradicting his professionalism.

You know - like that coach or teacher who always goes that extra mile for you, but, he can't really get into these types of conversations with you because of his role doesn't really create the space to do so. And to talk to kids about the opposite sex and dating with him usually follows the "company line" of "You should wait, you are too young to be dating" so on and so on. So, as any young person like yourself trying to find their way, you find yourself in a situation just like J. Cole discusses in his song Adolescences – where you low key look up to one of your homeboys or someone a little bit older than you – but the problem with that is just like the song says – he looks up to either you or someone else y'all age too... Which creates a situation like my Dad would say, "The Blind Leading the Blind" – he just as lost as you are and is navigating the world and these situations the same as you are. He has no concrete plan nor strategy for success. I am sure you can see how this leads to the unfortunate circumstances of teen pregnancy, STD's and other things that we will pick back up later in the Chapter on the Narrative and Womanizing.

So here you are struggling to figure out what to do and how to do it. No true guidelines or concrete idea as to how best to move forward, so you go into your room and you began to create this persona, this new you to deal with situations like this and others that keep happening and your skin isn't built for just yet. This version of yourself is the result of accepting The Narrative and becomes who you are and the way others will define your character.

OK let's stay here for a second... Think about how many people you know or your friends or even you – who preffers to be called by their nickname? This nickname is probably the invented character that represents them. Most people know somebody named Black, somebody named Snoop, somebody named Dre... Black is more than likely dark skinned and Black is what he was called by friends when they were roasting him. Now he has empowered that name and goes by it. He uses it with the girls, etc...

The point is, whether its Black, Snoop or Dre, these personas are different variations of the person who is being called or going by these names. I look at my friends and my boy "O" (from O Dawg in Menace II Society) is different than Rodney, A Sain is different from Aaron. My brothers Sherray and Ernest are different from Ray & EJ what they go by.

I don't want you to think that what I am saying is that this version of yourself is being fake or phony. I am a realist, keeping it 💯, this persona is necessary for survival. I am saying we need to examine who he is and how he operates. This "person" is constructed to defend you and shield who you really are from the ridicule and scrutiny of others. He also comes with SWAG and CONFIDENCE, he not only defends you from your boys but his swag has girls liking him.

Now that you have this new person to protect you from these feelings and interactions, you eventually become more aggressive and assertive in these situations. Before you know it, you find yourself in the position of promoting The Narrative to others because you have fully accepted this form of behavior and no longer question it. Nor do you feel awkward or uncomfortable when these situations happen.

Now, you're the one telling others they are soft, or whipped or anything else that promotes one of many Narratives that you once disagreed with. Being that you dealt with it and pulled through it, you never pause to think of how you are making others feel or even what they may be going through emotionally due to your words and actions.

In your mind, it isn't really that bad, you pulled through it. Since these behaviors have gained widespread social acceptance in some shape or form from others, you feel like it is a natural part of life. What makes this unnatural - is the feelings that you get when you were initially (first) confronted with The Narrative - and the fact that you had to develop a "persona" to handle these situations. Remember this: "Society has trained us to accept and never to question." I urge you to question this thought process and the actions that go along with it. Remember the Golden Rule is to "Do unto others, as you would have them do unto you." When we accept The Narrative, we find ourselves "Doing unto others what was done to us."

When we accept and play out this behavior, we are essentially programming and conditioning others into a process without ever considering their feelings or even greater, what are the long-term results of accepting The Narrative.

What's Wrong With The Narrative?

Stop…. Look around you… Take it all in… Look at the people who, "shoulda did this" and "coulda did that." Who do you see really, truly doing it? Who is really doing big things? Not many people. It's not that they did not want to do big things, or that something is "wrong" with their life. I am not saying that keeping a steady job and taking care of the responsibilities that you have created is a bad thing.

What I am saying is, doing just enough to get by, which is the life that most people are living is not what God has in store for you. True happiness is in being yourself and living a life that allows you to do what you are passionate about. When we accept The Narrative, we subconsciously (unknowingly) sacrifice time, energy and efforts that could have resulted in us realizing our potential and thus making our dream a reality. To further illustrate the point of What is Wrong With The Narrative, let's revisit our previous conversation with your boys…

Now the conversation is over, you all get back to playing 2k / Call of Duty. No big deal but in your mind, it's not truly over. You thinking about your girl now, like I said, you really rock with this girl, you like her, you respect her, this is Bae… So you thinking like, "Hey if she my girl and I am her guy, she gotta be feeling what I am feeling in terms of a physical attraction, right?" Plus, in your mind you thinking (wait for it…………..) "**EVERYBODY** else is doing it." Therein lies the problem – she rock with you because you are not everybody else – what's the biggest thing a guy your age has to do to get a girl?…. **CONVINCE HER THAT YOU ARE NOT LIKE ALL THE OTHER GUYS!!!** – Once you have went above and beyond to prove that you are different, then you good -she feeling you now… DUH!!! But no, this isn't what crosses your mind, what is of chief concern to you is that you have something to add to the conversation next time you and your boys are alone talking about girls.

So you find yourself either doing one of two things. 1 – you start putting this "pressure" on your girl to get a little more affectionate either, verbally or physically. If it is verbally, then you **"mistakenly on purpose"** lead the conversation on the phone or through text in that direction so you can see the reaction. If it is physically, you **"mistakenly on purpose"** put your hands in places when you all are joking and playing around just to see how she reacts. Either way you are not considering her feelings and the main reason that she was feeling you anyway – **YOU WERE DIFFERENT – YOU WERE NOT THE TYPICAL GUY** – now you have accepted the narrative and you feel this "pressure" (this is what the adults mean when they say peer pressure) to have something to add to the conversation and going against your natural judgment and how you genuinely feel, you began to pressure her. Or there is option 2 – which happens, more frequently than the first – you find another girl that is willing to do all these things and you have your way with her, when I was young we called this "being on the low" now it's called having a "side piece".

Let's look at this, you are now causing emotional stress on two young ladies all because you feel the need to save face in front of your boys and here is how. First, let's look at the "other girl", usually this girl is not considered the most attractive and rarely "gets the guy", she is the classic case of low self esteem. She has a long list of emotional issues that we will tackle at some other time, but the biggest thing is that she wants to be wanted and does not mind sacrificing her body because she has not been taught the value of her self worth. All she wants, even if momentarily, is the feeling of being wanted by someone. She doesn't mind if it is by someone who has a girl friend or if she never is publically acknowledged, she just wants to have that feeling. She is too young and immature to realize that she is being used.

Even if she does realize this, she feels the sacrifice is worth it because those needs of being wanted are being met in some fashion. Hopefully, at some point, down the road, this young lady will recognize her worth and which Narrative she has accepted and reject this role. However, there will be emotional scars that will linger and she will have to heal those wounds. When you stop to examine the role that you have played in her bruises, the question will be, was having something to add to a conversation among friends truly worth using someone that you have no emotional connection with?

The real you would say no it is not and feel remorse, I know because you paused, even if only for a split second to think about it. The persona you have created is the one looking to defend your short sighted actions…

***Now, to how you have hurt your girlfriend – I am sure this is much more obvious and self explanatory, you did her wrong by either cheating, or getting her to give up her innocence in any form or fashion. This pain cuts deep because she has done and stuck with what's right, more than most young ladies would or have to this point in their lives. She did her job of waiting and making sure that the guy she dated was a really good person before she gave him the time of day. Your persistence was rewarded and she slowly let her guard down and allowed you in. At first, you treated her with respect and dignity and you gave her the honor she deserves.

Now that you are feeling the pressure from your boys and you see the people around you doing more than what should be done at this age, you don't want to feel left out. So now you are pushing her and pressuring her and eventually she concedes but of course this is against her will. Slowly but surely you start to notice a small change in her behavior towards you and things aren't the same before you know it. You think it's her, but if you look at it, it's what you asked of her and what became of it she isn't feeling anymore so now you have created emotional scars on potentially two young ladies all to keep your boys from clowning you, which is something they were going to do anyways. This fella's, is what is wrong with The Narrative.

This was just one drawn out instance of what could potentially happen and how accepting the values and standards from others goes a long way to having damaging effects on people. I know some would say this is life and we have to learn to accept it. I say that it doesn't have to be. Why? Because there is no greater power than the **POWER OF CHOICE** – we all have it and we must understand its potential when we make decisions. You have the power to accept or Reject The Narrative. This was a look at what's wrong with the Narrative from the standpoint of how your actions can affect others. Let's look at how these actions affect you.

The Narrative & You

I know that the idea that you were designed and destined for greatness beyond measure is not one that you can see, since you are likely surrounded by poverty and mediocrity. Let's look at it like this, when you dreamed and imagined the life that you wanted, whether it was when you were a kid or even still to this day, how much does what you see effect that picture? Truthfully, not much if at all, we only place those limitations on ourselves when we begin to talk ourselves out of putting in the work to make our dream, our reality.

When it all boils down, accepting The Narrative, leads to Average and Mediocrity, which is not nor will it ever be what you were intended for. Being Average and Mediocre is not bad but it's not good either. Average people live with tons of regrets and find themselves drinking and smoking to cope with the thoughts of what could have been. I am not saying that something is wrong with that, what I am saying is that if you ask people who live with this reality they would be the first to tell you that this is not the life that they want you to lead. It wasn't their first choice either. If you ask yourself, do I really truly want to, work from 9 to 5 for 5 days a week, making just enough to pay my bills and take a vacation every now and again? I think that the answer is no. I will take it a step further; who do you see that is really HAPPY? Quick name me 5 people that you know that are Happy? Most people you know, complain of being tired, being worn out, mentioning bills, the list can go on and on.

I am not saying that rich people don't have problems, stress or their own set challenges that life has to offer. What I am saying is, if you lead a life that allows you to pursue your passion, then you will be a very happy and fulfilled individual. I believe that in order for you to find that piece of mind it begins with Rejecting The Narrative and being in control of your decisions and influence.

THE BIG PICTURE – What is the Narrative?

Solutions For Identifying & Rejecting The Narrative

Steps 1 – 3: HOW TO IDENTIFY THE NARRATIVE THAT YOU ARE BEING GIVEN:

Step 1: Ask yourself, What is being said to me?

Situation 1: Someone calls you a B-

Situation 2: Your boys clowning you for having genuine feelings for the girl you like.

Step 2: What I really hear when this is said to me?

Situation 1: He called me a B – so he is telling me that I am soft like a girl or I am not a man

Situation 2: If I were a real man, I would be in control of my girlfriend and she would be doing what I want her to; women should be controlled not respected

Step 3: The Way the Narrative Tells Me to React is to:

Situation 1: I have to fight this guy to prove that what he said is not true – my manhood must be defended

Situation 2: I have to find a way to make my girlfriend do things with me or I have to find another girl who will so that I can prove that I can control a woman and get what I want from one of them.

Steps 4 – 6 How To Reject The Narrative

Step 4: Will my actions or reactions get me closer to what I want out of life?

Situation 1: How does fighting or bullying someone because they called me out of my name get me closer to my dream or goals in life? If the answer is that doing this will not – then don't do it.

Situation 2: Is causing the emotional scars to young women worth having something to brag about to your friends? Let's keep it 💯… they are not going to stop being your friends because you don't have "experience" with girls – if they do, then you needed a better group of friends anyway so that's still a win for you.

Step 5: Think About How Your Actions Will Impact the Feelings of Other People

Situation 1: Fighting someone over roasting is not worth it, they gonna call my parents, his parents, the teacher has to write this up if this is at school, people watching could call the police if we are in public, all things that are not really worth jokes…

Situation 2: My girlfriend and or "The Other Chick" have feelings. I know that doing things to them so I can say I did, is not really worth them being upset and hurt because I wanted to bragg or just have something to talk about…

*** *Maturity is having the strength to express your feelings properly without hurting the feelings of others – Be Mature***

Step 6: Choose Your Actions

Situation 1: If you see things starting to get serious or you feel like things are about to go too far when you roasting, say "Look let's chill out before things get out of hand and I am not trying to go there." Remember whoever you were roasting with probably doesn't want to fight so somebody has to stop it before it starts. Finally, walk away, most people say "I wouldn't let them do me like that!" – well they are not going where you going anyway so don't worry about it.

Situation 2: Be happy with yourself and what you have… If you got a girlfriend and you really like her, tell your boys to be cool with the jokes because you like her. If they keep clowning then just answer "Yep I do" when they say all their jokes, eventually they will chill and respect your decision to treat your girl with respect.

*** I know these things are easier said than done – but remember there is no such thing as failure – only quitting – keep working and building the version of yourself that will make your dreams a reality. The version of you can be Dre, Snoop, Black, whatever you want to go by, just make sure that it is something you will forever be proud of…

Chapter 1
Discussion Questions

1.) <u>D.O.K. 1 Recall</u> Have you ever been put on spot or made fun of by your peers for something you said or did? Explain the emotions you felt while going through the situation.

2.) <u>D.O.K. 3 Evaluate</u> Reflecting on the situation you described in Question 1, do you think you responded appropriately? What were some of the determining factors in how you responded? Do you feel your response was influenced by what your peers think or feel?

3.) <u>D.O.K. 4 Analyze</u> Do you or someone you know prefer to go by a nickname? If so, what are some of the differences between the persona (your nickname) and who you know you (they) are?

4.) <u>D.O.K. 3 Recall</u> Have you ever had fun at someone elses expense to fit in with others who are considered popular or in the "In" crowd?

5.) <u>D.O.K. 4 Evaluate</u> Describe a situation where you tried to fit in whith your friends. Explain why you felt the need to not be left out, did the situation work in your favor?

Common Core Standards

CCSS RL 8.3 Analyze how particular lines of dialogue or incidents in a story or drama propel the action, reveal aspects of a character, or provoke a decision.

CCSS RL 9 - 10.3 Analyze how complex characters (e.g., those with multiple or conflicting motivations) develop over the course of a text, interact with other characters, and advance the plot or develop the theme.

CCSS RL 11 - 12.3 Analyze the impact of the author's choices regarding how to develop and relate elements of a story or drama (e.g., where a story is set, how the action is ordered, how the characters are introduced and developed).

Notes:

"The pressure to "fit in" when you are a young Black Male always seems to be very high. From wearing the "right" clothes and shoes to having a nice hair cut, the pressure doesn't stop. We must talk and act a certain way in hopes that we may escape the criticism or roasting from our peers. The constant hurdles we must jump over to get and stay accepted in our peer group feels endless. It is these "Narratives" that often prevent young black males from embracing who they truly are."

- Alan Gaines

Chapter 2:
Who Gives Us The Narrative

Ok, in order for us to accept or reject something, someone has to offer it first. So the question is who is offering this Narrative to you? Truth is, almost everyone has offered you "The Narrative" in some shape or fashion. The Narrative is given to us subconsciously by society whenever we have an interaction with something or someone and the response by that something or someone tells us that our behavior is either acceptable or unacceptable.

Here is one example from my personal experience: I was at a friends house one day and we were playing basketball I was in the 7th grade and everyone else was in the 8th. Now, to paint the picture and not to brag – I never went to school in my community, I was bussed across town to the school for gifted and talented kids. However, this particular day I wasn't too far from home and playing with one of the guys I had known because his older brothers and sister had went to school with my older brother and sister. So we over at his house playing basketball and I was good at basketball, I don't want to say I was on the verge of the NBA or anything but I could go – that's just keeping it 💯. Some of the people playing basketball that day knew of me but really didn't know me so to speak because I never went to school with them. I am killing – I mean we not getting off the court. We all know how most people get when they are losing, they had to start trash talking because they couldn't stop me on the court. So this particular day, I happened to be wearing some X Men shorts.

I remember going to the Village Shopping Center to get some clothes and my Dad saying explicitly, "Boy ain't nothing wrong with them shorts", when my mom picked them out for me. My initial reaction was that I didn't want them". The shorts were all red and had a black and yellow X Men logo on the bottom right side around the knee area. Oh they got to clowning me, "We know why you so good – it's because you are a Mutant!" I mean they went in on me. I got roasted pretty bad that day – it didn't affect the outcome on the court because – that was the only come back I had was to keep winning at that moment. But, and there is always a but, when I walked home, it was pretty lonely. I made up my mind on that walk that if it wasn't an acceptable brand name, I wasn't wearing it. I had accepted The Narrative, I was a brand junkie, like tons of other people in the world.

I was never one to have to have the top of the line most expensive thing, but shoes and clothes had to be by a reputable brand, if not, I refused to put it on my body because I never forgot how it felt to get roasted that day.

Ok, so here is a case of how I accepted The Narrative and eventually gave it. Now, let's fast forward to my Sophomore year in high school and now I have this new persona that will talk about others for not wearing brand name gear. One day, we are in Social Studies class and we roasting on this kid whom, it was pretty obvious that his family couldn't afford the brand name clothing that most people try to purchase for their kids. You know how it is, outside of those 3 or 4 good outfits you get at the beginning of the school year and that second set at tax time, for the most part kids who don't have it like that, are targets for the jokes. This particular classmate was a character of sorts, he was always attempting to be more than he obviously was, so he would lie about this or that. He even created a persona – he called himself Moffeoso – which was a play off of his last name – just to save face and try to fit in. He never really did but people knew his name, for the most part he was cool.

This particular day we were in class killing him. It started with him and another kid, but he was an easy target just like I was in those X Men shorts that day. Everybody is roasting him, girls laughing at him and even the teacher who is trying to keep us quiet has cracked a few smiles at some of the jokes. I will never forget the kid was wearing some BOFF jeans that day that were black but slowly fading gray with a BOFF jersey on. One of my classmates Dre said "What is BOFF? Does it stand for Better Off Flicking Fubu?" Bruh, we fell out laughing! He even laughed at that one! But when I looked at him, and it was one of those "gotta laugh to keep from crying" expressions on his face.

Looking back on it all these years later, I could have used my influence and popularity to keep things from escalating to that point. I don't know exactly how he felt that night when he was alone with just his thoughts. However, I can imagine that it wasn't too good of a feeling. I had been in those shoes with my X Men shorts, but I will admit that his was worse than mine. I am wrong for not having the courage of my convictions to stop everyone from clowning him but at that point in my life, I had accepted a Narrative and then I was giving it to others.

I urge you to remember the moments in your life that you were the butt of the jokes. Get reacquainted with those uncomfortable feelings and tap into those emotions. I know it isn't the best feeling in the world but ask yourself did you want someone to speak up for you in that moment? If you answered yes – that you wanted someone to speak up for you – then how bout you be the hero next time you and your friends, or just someone you know of is getting roasted. Gandhi – said "We must be the change that we would like to see in the world." Can you be that change?

More to the point, Narratives don't always come from outside individuals. More often than not, our families have the largest influence on us whether we know it or not. This can be both positive and negative. Here is another example of how I got a common narrative from my family.

I remember in 1st grade I had a girlfriend, she was very smart, had a great personality, she was cute and chubby. Now, I liked her a lot, she was very popular and I was too, so it was fitting that the "it girl" would be with the "it guy." Happy to have a "girlfriend" I am at my cousins house one day, now this cousin is about 8 months older than I am, and I bring a picture of the girl I have been telling him about for a while now so he could finally see how she looked. I give him the picture and immediately, he and his little brother begin laughing and run out the room and take the picture to my Uncle. At this point I am beginning to question if I gave them the right picture. I did, they were laughing because she was chubby. Right then and there I was given a Narrative that said that overweight women are undesirable. This Narrative was in direct contrast from the lesson that I was given from my Mother. Which was, that I am free to choose and love anyone based on the way that person makes me feel and how I feel about them. This choice is to be made free from how the person looks in outward appearance, I was perfectly cool with that, in fact that was why I chose her to be my girlfriend. However, my skin and resolve were not strong enough to withstand the feeling of embarrassment. I also thought that this means that I should never get a woman who is overweight by society's standards (although this is not how I thought about it at age 7 or 8) – The Narrative that I was given and I accepted went on to shape whom I dated in the future and how I treated people who dated overweight girls. Is this cool? NO! However, my cousins and Uncle gave me this Narrative and I accepted it.

These are just a few examples of who gives us The Narrative. Usually, The Narrative is given to us by people that are genuine and well intended individuals. A coach, a teacher, a relative, a friend, even a parent, can all give someone The Narrative. Let's look at a few other scenarios that may shape how we are given or give others The Narrative.

The obvious and most common culprit, or person responsible for giving The Narrative, is the rapper or entertainment figure. This idea and concept goes back well beyond the advent of rap music. Way back in the 50's and 60's the Great James Brown was a very large influence on the youth and his style of dress and hair was one that set The Narrative of that time. Today, we see this same concept of the "top rapper" or entertainer or athlete setting the trend that other guys follow.

I am not going to talk your ear off about this because we all know that what we see the rappers and ball players with and the girls drooling over, usually makes the decision for us in regards to fashion. While your parents bank accounts will determine how much of it that you can get. Sometimes it's the guy in the hood with the nice car and flashy clothes who you look up to – whoever it is – you know exactly what I am talking about. It's been this way for a very long time I'm sure and I understand that this will not change. We can however, think deeper about it.

Whether it's the Brand Name you are dying to put on or the girl you pass over because she couldn't be in the video but you really like her, at the end of the day you have to feel good about what you wear and who you date, no one else. If you are doing things to fit in, ask yourself, "What is it that I am trying to fit into?" Usually when you try to "fit" into something, you are not very comfortable when you finally do get inside – it's like squeezing an extra person in a car, everybody in but there ain't really enough space. You can't wait to get out and stretch.

I am saying, don't get in the car in the first place – Reject The Narrative that you "need" to ride – be comfortable and walk by yourself to the places you want to go in life.

THE BIG PICTURE: WHO GIVES US THE NARRATIVE

*** I can hear my mom saying to me – **Consider the source...*****
Today I give that same advice to you...

Solution 1: Think about who the person is that is giving you The Narrative?

- Is it a friend or another person around your age? If so what makes their way of thinking correct? Trust yourself more than you trust the words and thoughts of others. 💯

Solution 2: Don't Trust Others Blindly

- It may be someone in your family that loves you who is attempting to give you a Narrative. However, you have to look at what they have and where they are in their life.

- Is what they have and where they are – what you want and where you want to be? If the answer is no and what they are telling you doesn't seem or feel natural, then you must Reject The Narrative that they are giving you. What's ok for them doesn't have to be good enough for you – set your standards high and reach them.

Sometimes people you love, may not always know what's best, even though they love you.

The road to your destiny only has one set of footprints, the ones you will leave – don't be afraid to walk alone.

Chapter 2
Discussion Questions

1.) <u>D.O.K. 3 Analyze</u> Who are what influences the clothes or fashion trends that you or your peers are currently into? Do you feel pressure to dress or look a certain way? If so, why? How do you or your peers treat people who do not dress or look what others may feel is "acceptable"?

2.) <u>D.O.K. 1 Recall</u> Have you ever talked about or been talked about for clothes or shoes that you wore? If so how did it make you feel when you were talked about or if you talked about someone else, did you consider the feelings of the person you talked about?

3.) <u>D.O.K. 2 Explain</u> What physical characteristics are considered the standard of beauty? Where does this image come from? Is this a narrative that was given to you?

4.) <u>D.O.K. 3 Evaluate</u> Do you make decicisions about fashion and people you would date based on what your peers would think? If so explain why you felt the need to have your peers approval.

5.) <u>D.O.K. 2 Explain</u> Describe a situation in your life when you got advice on something from one of your peers. Did you ever question, how they got their information or did you just accept it?

Common Core Standards

CCSS RL 8.3 Analyze how particular lines of dialogue or incidents in a story or drama propel the action, reveal aspects of a character, or provoke a decision.

CCSS RL 9 - 10.3 Analyze how complex characters (e.g., those with multiple or conflicting motivations) develop over the course of a text, interact with other characters, and advance the plot or develop the theme.

CCSS RL 11 - 12.3 Analyze the impact of the author's choices regarding how to develop and relate elements of a story or drama (e.g., where a story is set, how the action is ordered, how the characters are introduced and developed).

Notes:

"Go to college so you can get a good job..." Consistently hearing statements to this effect, both at home and in school can add a lot of pressure to our youth. Living within the confines of the expectations of the adults in their life often results in the goals of the adults becoming the aspirations of the youth. Our job as adults must become to inspire the youth to develop their talents as well as instill within them the work ethic necessary to become great. Let's Be Mindful Of How What We Say Influences Those We Love..."

–Alan Gaines

Chapter 3:
Going To College and Getting A Job / Career Makes You Successful

To make this point I want you all to meet Justin.

Justin is a 16 year old sophomore. Justin stays with his mom. His father is somewhat in the picture, he knows him and he sees him from time to time but y'all know the story, Pops ain't there when he really needs him. (Which is all the time). So of course, Justin is dealing with issues of abandonment and is at the point where he just doesn't think about it and hopes the pain will go away. Moms is doing her best, she got a lil job that she goes to but they still on welfare. The most that Justin ever has in his house is just enough and that is not too often. Mom has a few on again off again boyfriends but nothing stable. One in particular, who is more on than off, Justin really can't stand because he stay arguing with his Moms. The yelling and cursing each other out is more of the norm and it stresses Justin out. Dude always getting drunk with his boys and seems to always find away to spend Moms money, which they don't have much of anyway. Justin can only look forward to getting new things 3 times per year. At the start of school, Christmas and tax time.

Justin is a bit of an awkward kid in regards to athletics, he can't really hoop, he wants to play football but the schools' team sucks and his mother didn't let him play pop warner as a kid because as she told him, she didn't want him to get hurt, yet the truth was she didn't have the money.

Nobody knows this, but Justin loves taking pictures, he always wanted a "real" camera but he never asked because he googled one a few years back and after seeing the price of it, he knew better than to ask. So he had a plan B, one day he was walking home and saw a billboard that read "Shot On An iPhone". The picture was amazing and Justin got to thinking, "I could do that!" So he begged his pops for an iPhone for his birthday and his dad bought him one. Now Justin was geeked, he no longer getting roasted for his Boost Incognito. (Shout out to my 5th grade class who used to clown me when I had mine) Now he can do a little bragging, but more importantly he can take the pictures of the things that he always admires on his walk home from the bus stop everyday after school.

Speaking of school, Justin is not the best student, but he tries. Justin struggles with reading, he sometimes gets a little confused when he doesn't know some words but he can follow for the most part. He wants to ask more questions in class but he don't want to get laughed at for what he feels maybe a dumb question. Justin is good in math, it comes pretty easy to him, however his Geometry teacher goes through the lesson pretty quickly and then gives a worksheet. Never really circulating the classroom making sure the students get it. He isn't truly confident in his abilities overall as a student and this is The Narrative he gets from his Mom and family:

> "You gotta get good grades and go to college!" "Go to school get your degree so you can get a good job because if you don't you gone be just another Nigga in the hood hanging on the block." "If you don't go to college then you gone be just like your Uncle D who still stay with Grandma." "You better get good grades because if you don't go to college, I don't know where you gone go... but you gotta get out my house" "Do you want to be like your Brother, he staying over there with your Auntie doing nothing... Why? Because he didn't do what he was supposed to do in school... Is that what you want?"

Justin is just like some of you... he thinks to himself:
> "College? Maaaan, I barely get this ish they teaching in High School, no way am I going off somewhere in those big ole classrooms so everybody can see how dumb I am."

Truth is, you know that you are not dumb. However, you hear a lot of conversations from older people and even teachers and the "smart" kids in your classroom and think... "What are they talking about, I'm lost" so you look around and it seems that everyone else is following along so you just try to blend in. In your mind, that college ish... is for the birds!... Justin thinks and feels the pressure but he's only a sophomore and while he can't see himself going off to college in 2 years, he has a little time because it's not time to make that "What you going to do with your life?" decision just yet... Plus being that Justin doesn't feel that he is the smartest kid in the world so when he hears his teachers say:

"You ain't gone never be anything" "I'm going to read about you in the newspaper one day…" "You gonna be dead or in jail if you keep this up" "These grades ain't gone get you to college"

Whether it is directed to him or someone else in the class, it only adds to the pressure he already is feeling. This isn't all that the teachers say but people with a negative outlook tend to hear the negative things that were said louder than the positive things.

This society, especially in the hood, puts an enormous amount of pressure on you to go to college and be successful. The Narrative that you are given is pretty clear: If you don't go to college then you will be a failure.

This is so far from the truth, yet you constantly hear or live with this pressure every day.

Justin has dreams of opening a studio of his photography one day. He tries to block out the noise that his life is going to be defined by going to college. He wants to learn how to capture the world he sees with a camera. Unfortunately, he goes to a school much like yours, which is more than likely underfunded, with little to no budget for things like photography club, debate club, robotics and journalism. Since he is not an athlete, it's no extra curricular activities for Justin.

Sound familiar? I know it does, too familiar, Justin's passion and potential are going to waste because everyone is telling him what he is supposed to do. No one is asking nor encouraging what he wants to do with his life. Justin spends hours after school and on the weekend taking pictures with his iPhone. Justin's cloud is nearly filled with images that only he has seen because he has no outlet for his passion and he feels alone and unable to tell anyone about his affinity, (love) for taking pictures because his boys will clown him and girls will laugh. In the hood no one sees the masculinity in taking pictures, which is why Justin feels that he must conceal his passion. So now the question becomes will Justin accept The Narrative? First let's talk for a quick second…

Lil' Bro trust me I know how you feel about school… I am a teacher. I have taught grades 5 -12 and I graduated from College and I have a Masters Degree. Let me be the 1st to apologize to all my former students who I ever gave the impression that you have to go to college to be successful. I know that what I am saying and what I am about to say flies in the face of what you hearing from pretty much everyone; your parents, your teachers, your coaches, whoever has some type of influence on you, has pretty much pushed the mentality of College = Success. *That is not necessarily true.* Ok so let's get this straight before I go further – *School is A way to be successful. School is not THE ONLY way to be successful. School is likely a road you have to go through to get to success, but that only depends on what you want out of life.*

I could rattle off a lot of ultra successful people who never went to or dropped out of college. On the flipside I can also show you a lot of college grads that are struggling to make ends meet. *Life is about living out your purpose, while making a living from your passion…* 💯

We adults have to be more mindful of what message we are sending to all students when we say certain things to them. Most of what we are saying is unfair on many levels because 9 times out of 10 the person that is giving you this Narrative, whether parent or teacher, has not truly taken the time out to make sure that you know how to do the work. Nor have they found you the resources to make sure that you are properly prepared for college. Instead, they just tell you what you better do, never once thinking that you may not know how to do the work. Don't get me wrong, I know that these people genuinely care about you and want what's best for you. However, you have to understand that your parents and loved ones have also accepted this Narrative, that school and college is *"The Way"* to success. They were given it and now are passing it on to you. Remember, society trains us to accept and never to question. We haven't questioned this mentality for generations or the amount of people who have accepted this Narrative and destroyed their lives because of the pressure that has been placed on them.

You are probably thinking Destroyed? What you mean destroyed? Well let's check back in on Justin to find out how the pressures of this Narrative can lead someone to destroy their own life…

Ok, so while you were letting me talk to you, Justin was growing up… Now he is a 17 and at the end of his Junior year and he knows that all the pressure of "What you gonna do after college?" is coming as he is about to begin his senior year in a few months. Summer break is approaching and his mother has already been on his neck about getting a job, because as she puts it he is "Too old to keep begging for money every time I look up, you need to get your butt a job!" Justin doesn't mind working, he cool with that but he wants to take his pictures and build his portfolio. Tired of hearing this all day and all night, Justin starts hanging out later and later as summer approaches in hopes that his mom is either sleep or ready to go to sleep by the time he gets back in.

It's graduation night for a lot of his Justins' boys who are Seniors, and he is going out to celebrate with some of them from the neighborhood. They got a hotel room and you know the scene people stopping through all night just chillin'. One of the people who roll in is the hommie Money. He got the name because he always been into Hustling since they were little shorties. His real name is George, but you know you can't get out the hood without a nickname so when George accepted "The Narrative" he started telling people to call him Money. Money, comes through the hotel tonight with a QP of dro and its bout to get lit. Justin has never gotten high before and his friends have always respected this decision and never really pressed him on it. "Hey that's more bud for me" as they saw it. Tonight, Justin is thinking really long and hard about blazing up and just saying "F it all."

You see lately, his grades have began to slip a little bit and he has been getting detention for talking back to the teachers. His behavior is taking a step back but overall, it isn't something that he could not control if he wanted to. Truth is, he not really feeling school that much any more. It's not that school is bad but he is a quiet dude and all the attention goes to the "really smart" kids or the "athletes" and since the perception of him doesn't check either box, he sits through those 8 hours 5 days a week with his mind on other things.

I mean his teachers are cool, don't get me wrong and they try but majority of his teachers are young white Teach For America teachers that are in the profession to pay back a student loan and not really vested, or deeply concerned in what is going on in his neighborhood. The other teachers are too old and don't really relate to his world, they don't like rap and they always on the kids about how they dress or their hair. There is Mr. Red and Mr. Long, everybodies 2 favorite teachers. They are always there for their students but Justin been going through it and since everyone is always all over Mr. Long & Mr. Red – they always seem to be super busy and Justin feels like they won't have time to talk to him.

Justin is dying to ask them for a way to get into photography because he really loves it, that is all he thinks about, I mean it is burning in his chest and he NEEDS TO EMBRACE THIS PASSION! It drives him crazy that he has to hide it because he knows his boys will clown him, his mom is only worried about him going to college or getting a job – whichever gets him out of her house first (if she get him through high school then she feels that she has done her job) – his Pops still call or come through every once in a while but it's more talking "AT" – Justin about "being a man" than it is Justin being able to share with him his feelings. All this is racing threw his head as liquor and weed is circulating the room and the temptation is growing by the second…

So as Justin sits in this hotel room and Money is rolling up this blunt and about to pass it around Justin is sitting there thinking:
Do I say: "F&$K it" let me hit the weed and throw all my potential and dreams away because I know if I start smoking now I probably ain't gone finish school and if I do finish school – that college ish… Is definitely out the window… - I can just get a lil job stack some bread and move out in about 6 months – just be on my own… "

Or do I say: "I'm good – you know I don't smoke – and just go tell Mr. Red or Mr. Long that I really need to talk to them and it's super important – when I get back to school on Monday and see how they can help me with my photography? Either way, Justin is next in the circle and after his boy O takes his pull, he knows he gone ask him if he wants to hit the weed. Justin is thinking… "Man, O just finished here comes the blunt" O leans over to Justin and offers him the blunt – Justin takes a deep breathe – looks at it and says….

What happened next is beside the point... The question is what would you say? What would you do? This situation, we can't forget is being brought on by the pressures from The Narrative of College Equals Success. If Justin was not being constantly harassed with these Narratives of college and school and grades – he would not find himself looking for a way to escape the pressures of the expectations. Nor the feelings of guilt and failure if he doesn't achieve it. If what you want out of life requires that you go to college and get good grades, then by all means you should be busting your butt trying to get straight A's. However, if it doesn't, then you should still be busting your butt trying to get straight A's! Why? Because you should try to do the very best in everything that you do! You can't turn greatness, (which is what you should be trying to reach) on and off.

I want you to find your passion as quickly as possible and begin to pour all of your time and efforts into making sure that you are making that passion your reality. Take every step towards that goal, map out a plan of how you are going to do it. Discipline yourself in everything that you do, from washing the dishes and sweeping the floor to turning in every assignment in class. Your passion may not require a college degree. And if that's the case then when you are done with your school work – do the lonely work as my man Fletch puts it. Play your guitar until you need new strings, dance everyday until you physically can't move anymore, learn to code the next great app, whatever it is – Reject The Narrative and Write Your Own Script... 💯

The BIG PICTURE
How To Flip The Script and Control The Pressure You Feel

Step 1: Find your passion

Everyone has something that they love to do and it may come easy to you. It's probably the thing you find yourself always thinking about and something you could do everyday all day and be happy. You feel very good when you do it and you probably are better than most people who do it. I used Justin's love of photography as an example of a passion in this chapter. What is yours? What fire is burning in your chest and keeps you up all night thinking about it? Whatever your answer is – that is your passion! Embrace it Fam…

Step 2: Be Vocal About It!

Justin could have changed The Narrative that he heard by simply speaking up and letting everyone know about his love for photography. Keeping it 💯 – all the adults in your world just want you to do something positive, they really don't care what it is that you do. They just want it to be positive. If you or Justin in this case, would just speak up about what you are passionate about, you will find that most people will support it. You may get some jokes about it at 1st but once everyone sees that you are serious – they are going to leave you alone. Before you know it… You will have Flipped The Script!

Step 3: Stay With It! - Don't Let Anyone Write Your Script

Ok , I created Justin from a lot of young men that I have taught or mentored and I know that a lot of you felt what he was going through. I want to point out the fact that Justin hid his passion, he did this because he worried about what most people would say about him. Bro, you can't let no one write your script. Let me tell a quick true story to make this point final.

My very 1st year teaching I had this student named Robert Foster. I was teaching 7th grade and Robert had a history of being in trouble in school and was behind academically. He had that dog though and I saw it early – he tried extremely hard at everything. So one day I told the students that in order to be successful they had to know what they wanted out of life, so their homework was to come to school the next day with what they wanted to do with their life.

So the next day, I am going around asking everyone what is their life goals, of course I got Doctor, Lawyer, NBA etc… I get to Foster and he says, "I want to be a Pastry Chef, I want to bake cakes." One of the students said, "Dang Foster, you gone be a stay at home Mom and bake cookies." Everyone busted out laughing… It was funny – I will admit. Foster would later tell me, at that moment his dreamed was crushed… Being the teacher, I jumped right in on everyone laughing and said, "I don't know why y'all laughing, he has a better chance at being a Pastry Chef than some of y'all do at making it to the NBA, Foster if that is what you want, then don't let nobody stop you!" Robert said "Okay Mr. Gaines". Robert Foster graduated with a 4.0 from Culinary Arts School and is currently… A PASTRY CHEF. Write your own script – Don't be an actor…

Robert Flipped The Script and is living his dreams…

Chapter 3
Discussion Questions

1.) <u>D.O.K. 3 Evaluate & Analyze</u> Do you feel pressure to go to college? If so, why?

2.) <u>D.O.K. 2 Evaluate</u> Do you think you are prepared for college?

3.) <u>D.O.K. 2 Explain</u> Do you have a talent or passion that you hide because what you think others would think about it?

4.) <u>D.O.K. 3 Analyze</u> Compare and contrast your life and school to Justin's life and school.

5.) <u>D.O.K. 3 Evaluate</u> If Justin smoked the marijuana at the end of the story who would you blame? Discuss the role you think his parent, his teachers and Justin has in the decision he makes.

6.) <u>D.O.K. 4 Create</u> What would you do if you were Justin and why?

Common Core Standards

CCSS RL 8.2 Determine a theme or central idea of a text and analyze its development over the course of the text, including its relationship to the characters, setting, and plot; provide an objective summary of the text.

CCSS RL 9 - 10.2 Determine a theme or central idea of a text and analyze in detail its development over the course of the text, including how it emerges and is shaped and refined by specific details; provide an objective summary of the text.

CCSS RL 11 - 12.2 Determine two or more themes or central ideas of a text and analyze their development over the course of the text, including how they interact and build on one another to produce a complex account; provide an objective summary of the text.

Notes:

Accepting The Narrative...

Section 2:

Examining How Young Males Use The Scripts of Society As A Crutch To Avoid Taking Accountability

"A Fatherless Generation has led to a New Generation of Fathers who are supplying their children with all the missing pieces..."

- Alan Gaines

Chapter 4:
If My Daddy Was Here… Everything Would Be Alright With Me

Alright, this is the chapter that most of you are going to be able to relate to. I know first hand how not having your Pops around can mess with your head. I dealt with this personally for 23 years of my life and in some ways to this very day. No, we didn't build this relationship when I became 23 either. That just happened to be how old I was when I got over it. Now, before I go on, I got a father, he just is not my biological father. Ernest Stansil has been there for me since my mom was pregnant with me. His influence on my life has a whole lot to do with me writing this book for you…

Ok, so you're probably wondering, what made me get over it after 23 years? Quite frankly, my biological father, Albert Gaines, and what he said to me on July 20, 2005 forced me to realize things that I never even considered. Before we get to that day let me give you a little background about me and immediate family.

Keeping it 💯 – my Moms was 13 years old when she got pregnant with my older brother Sherray and 14 when she had him. If that wasn't enough, shortly there after she was pregnant again at 14 years old with my sister Shellerray and 15 when she had her. Yeah you read that right, Sherray was born January 2, 1978 and Shellerray was born January 12, 1979. My mom was a freshman in High School with 2 kids. Oh yeah, Sherray and Shelley got 2 different fathers. This fact was the reason I never clowned a girl for being "out there" – or what y'all consider a "thot". My Moms wasn't a "thot" but I am sure guys probably thought she was easy because she was 15 with 2 kids. But hey, as my Mom would say all the time when we tried to judge others, "You don't live on my street". She told me this over and over and to always consider what you don't see when you look at someone… Fella's let's pump our brakes on all that name calling of girls, what she going through or has been through just might break your heart if you knew what has been done to her… Bro, you don't live on her street – these sisters got it super hard out here fam and we clowning them, that ain't right, check y'all selves for real – let little Mama breathe – she trying to figure life out just as much as you are … Her Daddy gone like yours is. Bro she got Narratives that she must Reject as Well!!!

Ok, I am off my soap box… But it had to be said…

The grace of God is the only way I can imagine how anyone can endure what Mom's had to go through. She never, ever made any excuses or bad mouthed any of our fathers. I followed shortly after she graduated from High School, she had me at 19 and I have a different father than my older brother and sister. So my Mom was a single teenage mother of 3. Mom's kept it real whenever we asked questions about our Daddies, some would said she kept it too real. When I was 16, I had the courage to start asking about my biological or as we used to call it, my sperm donor. I asked Moms, what happened to their relationship and she told me flat out:

> "Albert and I were never together, he was my friend. He would look out for me, take me where I needed to go because I didn't have a car at the time. We would hang out but were never together. One night, we were drinking and started fooling and one thing led to another. It wasn't the first time we did but it turns out I got pregnant that night. And just because we were not together doesn't mean that he should not have been in your life, I never stopped him from being there for you. It was my choice to lay down with him that night and his choice to not be in your life. A man should take care of his responsibilities – and Albert chose not to take care of his responsibility. I want you to know something, Alan, through all this, I want you to know that nothing is wrong you – this was his choice –God don't make no mistakes baby, ok…

I responded yes and she gave me a really big hug and kissed me on my cheek. That settled my emotions for the moment and I felt better inside. But it did nothing about the pain I had when I looked in the mirror and I didn't see my moms reflection. I don't look like her and I didn't know how he looked and that always bothered me. It was cool but it didn't make those nights that I was up in my room crying thinking about him. It did nothing for me as I would sit in the back of my homeboy Rodney's van and watching him and his dad interact, taking notes in my head of things I can't wait to do with my son. Simply put Mom's words gave me clarity but I still had the pain of what my life would be like if I knew who my father was and if he were in my life…

Ok, so what happened to me on July 20, 2005 that made me get over it. So, I told y'all I was always pretty (very) smart. The summer going into my Senior year of college I was 1 of 10 people selected for a research internship @ the Schaumburg Library in New York. On this particular day, the speaker was Herb Boyd, he was going through his presentation about how the internet was making information from everywhere more accessible. This concept was rather new in 2005. So he is talking and he said that you can find anyone you want, all you have to do is google search them. Hearing this, both my mind and that empty place inside got to going crazy… I completely missed the rest of his presentation because all I could think of at that time was trying to find Albert. So, as the day goes on and our work for the day is done, I hurry back to the dorm we were staying in so I could pull out my laptop and get to searching for Albert Gaines.

The whole ride home I am thinking about how I am about to cuss this nigga out. In my head I am thinking how the conversation is going to go, "Do I start the conversation off calling him a Bi%&#?" You know I got to call him a B---- what other word do we got to make them feel the pain we going through? I don't know, but I do know that I am about to go in on this nigga soon as he get on the phone… So I'm ready for this. So I get to the room, I pull out the laptop and google Albert Gaines and……… 18 different Albert Gaines pop up on white pages dot com.

Bro, I came this close, I had to finish the deal, so I wrote all 18 numbers down in my notebook and got to calling each one. I went "0 for 11" to start. However on the 12th call, a woman answered and seemed surprised to hear someone asking for Albert Gaines, the voice was of a older woman, mid to late sixties early seventies at best. She said with such a sweet voice, *"Baby, Albert is dead." "Who is this calling for him anyway?"* A little shook by the news, I stuttered trying to reply and before I could get my name out, the voice replied, *"Is this Alan?"* I could only say *"yeah"* with a confused tone. My mind began to wonder how or even why would he be dead, hearing nothing coming from my end of the phone, the voice said, *"This your grandma, Dimples."*

I almost breathed a sigh of relief, because I figured that the Albert she was talking about was my Grandfather and not my biological father, being that I knew Dimples was my paternal grandfather's second wife. This too, was weird and uncomfortable because I didn't pause to grieve for him and for so long, probably out of anger, I told myself that it mattered not to me if Albert was dead. So, hearing that he was, left me tripping for a second. I wasn't even thinking about him dying, I wanted answers. Dead men don't talk and if he was dead I would have to live with questions that messed with my head for the rest of my life. It's ironic, that as I am writing this I found that I am yet to have grieved for my grandfather and I had more of a relationship with him then I did Albert. I don't want to seem heartless, but my sentiment was just like 2 Pac's:

"He passed away / and I didn't cry / because my anger / wouldn't let me feel for a stranger"

My sights were on Albert only, so Dimples, gave me a number to call to get Albert's number, which I did. So the moment was here and I am ready to call him. I called my wife, who was my girlfriend at the time and clicked over and dialed Albert… So I dial the number and in my head I'm ready to go in on him. After about the 3rd ring someone picks up, it was a woman so I asked for Albert. She sounded a little puzzled, when she said *"He is not here, can I take a message?"* I said *"yeah – tell him Alan called."* She said *"Alan? His son Alan?"* I said, *"I wouldn't call myself his son, cause he ain't never been my father, but yeah… That Alan"*

I'm thinking "Oooooohhhhh I told her! Pumping out my chest because I gave her a little piece of what I am going to give Albert. Bruh, she didn't have nothing to do with it, but I am so gassed up – I'm like anybody can get it at this point!

She told me that he would be back in about 30 minutes and I could call back at that time because he would be home then. I gave him an hour because I didn't want to keep playing phone tag. I was ready to speak to buddy, so I could go off. So I call back an hour later with Carla on the phone and the same woman answers the phone and when I ask to speak to Albert, she says *"Hold on, let me get him"* … From the other end of the phone, I heard him say *"Hello"*

So as he is saying this, I am trying to bring all my swag and toughness into my throat so I can sound super hard when I replied, "Yeah... This Alan" – low key I am nervous on the inside but we ain't face to face so I gotta act hard because although this is feeling weird, the moment is here now! So let's get it! So here is how the convo went:

Albert: *So wsup?*

Me: *You tell me wsup?*

Albert: *Nothing I guess...* (I could hear in his voice that he was shook – couldn't run no more – Coward!)

Me: *What you mean nothing? You the one with the explaining to do – so where you been?* (I am heated and I am sure he can hear the hostility {rage} in my voice)

Albert: *What you mean where I been?*

Me: *Where you been since the last time I seen you and you walked out my life?*

OKAY – LISTEN WHAT HAPPENS NEXT BRO – ON MY MAMA – YOUR NOT READY FOR BUT HERE IT GOES.

Albert: *Man, I been pimpin hoes and slammin Cadillac dose (doors)...*

What the (bleep)!!! Is what I was thinking. I can't make this up... I SWEAR TO GOD that is what he told me, I honestly don't know even remember how the conversation ended.

All I could think about in that moment was how my Mama was soooo right that day when she said, GOD DOESN'T MAKE ANY MISTAKES... Because right then, I knew that God loves me so much, that he did not allow someone of such low character to be around to be in my life to influence me in what would have obviously been a negative way.

I sat up in that room that night and was finally relieved. All I could think about is - if he was the example I would have look up to, I would be a very F'd up individual 💯. I know without a doubt that I would not be sitting here right now writing this if he was in my life. That night I slept real good because I let it go. I stopped holding on to it – I realized that I was giving those thoughts power simply because I was thinking them and letting them control me. I didn't want to take accountability for things I was doing, so I would blame him and he was an easy target… That day I thanked God for removing him from my life and placing Ernest in my life and kept it pushing.

I'm going to give you the message my mom gave me:
I want you to know that nothing, and I do mean nothing, is wrong with you. If your Pops is dead or locked up, then that's a different story in regards to why your Pops isn't around. However, if my mans is out there somewhere and is not in your life, IT IS BECAUSE OF CHOICES THAT HE MADE AND IT HAS NOTHING TO DO WITH YOU OR YOUR MOM. If he truly, truly, truly wanted to be there for you, he would have and that is real. I am fully aware that circumstances will take not only our fathers away but also as other men we may look up to and see as father figures but how long can you use that excuse? Bro – I dealt with that pain, so I know it hurts but the truth is – THE WORLD DON"T CARE THAT YOUR POPS IS GONE…

Bro, I know that may seem a little insensitive (harsh) or savage as y'all say, but it doesn't. I care that you going through that pain – I empathize (feel) 100% with what you dealing with – I cried twice writing this chapter! But if we keeping it 💯 – ain't no teacher going to say –"I am going to give you an A because your Dad isn't around." Ain't no job application got a space for you to write in if your Dad was around or not. So you gotta find a way to deal with the pain and still conquer your world.

You have to Reject This Narrative that "If my Pops was around then everything would be alright with me." Everything's already – alright with you! The problem is – how you are choosing to look at yourself because of this situation. Look, it's too many examples of people who overcame not having their Pops around who went on to do super big things. You can too! I am pretty sure everyone of those people who went on to have success in spite of not having their father around dealt with that fact emotionally on their road to success.

Remember this – I can't give you nothing if your hands are full… You got to put what you are holding down in order to catch what is coming your way. Bro, you could be missing out on major things because of this Narrative that you have accepted as the reason for what is going wrong in your life.

Another thing, you have to appreciate the life you have and the things that you do have. It may not be much but it is something, take care of it and cherish what you have. You can't improve your life if you don't care about it. I know that not having your Dad can make you feel like "Don't nobody care about me – so why should I care about others?" You can not prosper (become better) if you don't love yourself. You may not recognize that you don't love yourself. However, a lot of the anger and frustrations that you are holding onto because your Dad is not in your life, has evolved into feelings of emptiness and doubts of your self worth.

As you can see from my encounter with my biological Pops, this Narrative that "If my Dad was in my life…" maybe a blessing in disguise, you never know? If he isn't the type of person who is willing to take care of his responsibilities, then is that the type of person you would want to follow? I don't think so…

Look Lil' Bro, 1st love yourself by looking in the mirror and believing that you are enough and worthy to be loved. 2nd Let go of the excuse that your Dad's absence is to blame for your problems – you have to take accountability for yourself and your actions – God has given you everything and everyone that you need in your life, recognize that and get to work on taking charge of your life. The sooner you realize that you have empowered this Narrative and you can't control what your Pops does, you will begin to accept responsibility for your actions and begin changing your world.

THE BIG PICTURE
Flipping The Script On My Daddy Not Being Here

Look, I can't tell you how to feel about your situation with your Dad, if he isn't in your life, for whatever reason. Trust me, some people have their Dad and wishes he wasn't around. That's real. I am not going to sit here and act like not having my biological father in my life didn't affect me, it did. For whatever reason that your Pops isn't there, I can't speak to that but let me say this 1st, to help you get the point I am making. Here is something one of my teachers Mrs. Vincent made us memorize in the 7th grade:

Excuses are the tools of the incompetent, which build monuments out of nothing. And those who specialize in them, seldom become good at anything else.

All that means is, your excuse no matter how valid (real) is still an excuse. Stop worrying about what you can't control and focus on that which you can! **YOUR LIFE** is in **YOUR HANDS**!!! I know it hurts, I know there is pain, I know you want answers, but you can't stop and wait for them!

Think about this, if you had everything you wanted in regards to your Pops, I mean if you could make everything the way you wanted it, wouldn't you do your very best at everything? If he was there, wouldn't you pay attention in class, wouldn't you try your hardest and be respectable? If you answered yes and you probably did, then why not do that without him? Wouldn't that be what he would want from you?

Bottom line fam – *Do What You Got To Do... No Excuses*

Chapter 4
Discussion Questions

1.) <u>D.O.K. 2 Apply</u> Why do you think the author wanted to find his biological father?

2.) <u>D.O.K. 3 Evaluate</u> How do you think the authors Mother's honesty helps him deal with teh absence of his biological father?

3.) <u>D.O.K. 4 Create</u> The author states that he realizes his biological father would have been a negative influence on him do you agree? Use textual evidence to support your answer.

4.) <u>D.O.K. 3 Analyze</u> The author states that he had to began taking accountability and stop blaming his biological father in order to grow as a person. Do you agree with that? Why or why not?

5.) <u>D.O.K. 4 Create</u> The author encourages you to appreciate the life that you have, do you appreciate life? If so, what are you doing to show that you appreciate your life?

Common Core Standards

CCSS RL 8.3 Analyze how particular lines of dialogue or incidents in a story or drama propel the action, reveal aspects of a character, or provoke a decision.

CCSS RL 9 - 10.3 Analyze how complex characters (e.g., those with multiple or conflicting motivations) develop over the course of a text, interact with other characters, and advance the plot or develop the theme.

CCSS RL 11 - 12.3 Analyze the impact of the author's choices regarding how to develop and relate elements of a story or drama (e.g., where a story is set, how the action is ordered, how the characters are introduced and developed).

Notes:

OR

"I once heard that 'Art used to immitate life, now Life immitates Art.' This reversal in what was a common principle has led to a generation who is losing sight of what it means to be authentic."

- Alan Gaines

Chapter 5
Everybody Doing It, I Should Be Too…

I don't know how many times I heard my parents say, "If they jump off a bridge are you going to jump with them?" I honestly thought that was a saying that my parents made up until I heard it on a commercial a few years back. However, between my older brother, Sherray, my older sister Shellerray and myself, I am pretty sure I heard this repeated at least 1 million times. This was my parents' way of telling us not to be followers. Let me give you the same message, don't be like everybody else.

Ok, look at it like a pair of Jordan's. We all know that a pair of J's has a release date right? Why? They have a release date because only a limited amount of new J's are made. So, if you don't get up and get in line for them when the store opens they are going to be sold out and you will not get your pair. This is also why J's are so expensive, not a lot of people will get that chance to get a pair. I want you to begin to think of yourself in the same way, be more exclusive. You don't see everybody walking around with a new pair of J's on, you see some people with them on. Don't be a pair of Huaraches when you can be some Bred 11's. My point is, why be like everybody else when you can be who everyone wants to be like?

Let me stay on the shoes for a minute to make this point. Think about a pair of Huaraches for a second. You see everybody wearing Huaraches, in just about every color. Why? It's a nice looking shoe, it is priced high enough where everyone respects them. You can wear them with a lot of different outfits and at the end of the day it is a comfortable shoe. Nothing wrong with Huaraches, I like them keeping it 💯. But they not them Wolf Grey 5's though… I'm just saying… Check it out, when you get them new J's, you also have to go get a new outfit to go with the J's. They don't go with any and everything you got in your closet. Them J's are exclusive, that's why when you see most people rocking them, it's a big event like homecoming or some type of event where everyone gone be there. Them Huaraches on the other hand, people wear those to school everyday. Bro, be exclusive.

Look, if this is going over your head, then google what you don't understand and you will see the point that I am making very clearly. So let's get back to it. Keep it 💯 - Do you see stores in the hood selling Fake Huaraches? I don't, but I do see them selling fake J's. I see websites selling fake J's. I'll say it again, don't be like everybody else… Be who everyone wants to be like…

You gotta switch up that mindset and start thinking for yourself, or as my mother would say, "Be a leader, not a follower." As a teacher, I get so tired of hearing, this wasn't fair or that wasn't fair. In the words of my Daddy, "Life ain't fair, deal with it." I want y'all to get out of this mindset that you deserve what everyone else has. Or that you should do what everyone else is doing. Now the question is, do you want to go where everyone else is going? Do you want out of life what everyone else wants out of life? NO - YOU WANT WHAT YOU WANT!!! You have your own dreams but trust me Lil' Bro, you will never get to those dreams by driving down the path everyone else takes.

Take a second and look around at the people older than you. Most of them had the same mindset that you have right now when they were your age. Most people went with the flow and did what everyone else was doing and what did that get them beyond a job that they are complaining about? I'm just keeping it real with you. 90% of the people you know that are adults are either fronting on social media and or just making enough money to meet all their needs. They take a vacation from time to time just to life it up. But in between post and pics, they getting up 5 days a week going to a job that they are probably over qualified for and smarter than their boss. Yet they still complaining about the B.S. they have to deal with at work. How do I know? Because I am in that position right now! My self and plenty of others are those Huaraches - you know, look nice, expensive enough, and comfortable.

Don't trip I won't be in this position too much longer, but I had to switch up my mindset in order to get out of it. I am trying to get you to change yours before you get into it. Don't get me wrong, I am not knocking how other adults live their lives, but I don't want you to be content with just enough. You deserve more and the very best of everything you want. I am about to be those Wolf Grey 5's and Bred 11's. I want you to be some too.

Why Most People Want To BE Like Everybody Else?

I could give a lot of reasons why most people want to be like everybody else. However, the most obvious reason? They don't want other people talking about them in a negative way. Just being all the way real, no one wants to feel left out. It makes you feel worthless and plain bad about yourself. I get that point and I understand your motivation to not feel left out. However, that comfort of being like everyone else doesn't provide the direction that you are going to need to make your goals your reality.

What I am saying to those of you who want to be like everybody else is this; Due to the fact that you will never be in control of what everyone likes, then you are not taking control of your life nor are you working towards your goals. With someone else dictating the styles and trends you are losing valuable time you could be putting into perfection of your craft.

Being that trends and styles change so fast, you are always going to be a little behind on something and eventually, you are going to find yourself spending time researching to find out what it is that everyone is talking about or doing. Oh my bad, nowadays it is called "going viral." So between watching the latest viral video, figuring out what and how to use the newest saying, (we turnt, that's lit and I'm savage - just to name a few) and dressing in the latest style, you tell me when and where are you going to have time to take control of your goals and dreams?

The Big Picture
It Is Okay To Do You

I know that it can be lonely, doing your own thing. People going to hate or talk bad about you for the moment but when they see they can't break you, eventually they will respect you. Stick to your grind, before you know it you will begin to get comfortable and accept that you are different and going places that everyone will not go. So, if you are going to be that pair of Carmine 6's, that everyone wants but few people get, then you got to do what it takes to get them. Let's look at the process of buying some Jordan's figuratively and see how to apply that process literally:

You have to have the money to buy the shoes - people get paid from the work they do, I want you to put in the time and effort on your skill or craft, you put the work in you will have the money.

Get up early - Don't sleep in and think your goals are going to take care of themselves, sorry, life doesn't woker like that. You are not the only person that wants to be the best at what you want to do, so you have to beat them to the spot. Get up early and grind towards your goals! Daily - If you are faithful over few, you will be ruler over many!

Drive to the store - Take the right roads and paths to get to the place in life where you will get the opportunity to have what you want. J's ain't sold at every store, your dreams ain't hanging on every corner either. You are going to have to know exactly where you want to go in life in order to obtain your goals and dreams. Success is something that is planned 1st and then you have to work achieve it.

Huaraches on the other hand, the price ain't too bad so it won't take too much to get the money, you get up when you want to because they are always in stock and just about every shoe store has them so you don't have to have a particular store to get them.

Flip The Script and be a Retro Pack...

Chapter 5
Discussion Questions

1.) <u>D.O.K. 2 Explain</u> What do you think of when you see a pair of New Jordans? Why do you think the author encourages you to view yourself the same way?

2.) <u>D.O.K. 3 Analyze</u> The author says he likes Huaraches, so why does he encourage you to not to be like them?

3.) <u>D.O.K. 4 Evaluate</u> Why is it important to be exclusive in your thoughts and how you carry yourself?

4.) <u>D.O.K. 3 Analyze</u> The Jordan brand represents excellence or a high standard, have you ever considered what your name represents to other people? Do you ever think about how you can influence what others think about you?

5.) <u>D.O.K. 4 Create</u> Describe the work/effort the author states it takes to be like a pair of Jordans.

Common Core Standards

CCSS RL 8.1 Cite the textual evidence that most strongly supports an analysis of what the text says explicitly as well as inferences drawn from the text.

CCSS RL 9-10.1 Cite strong and thorough textual evidence to support analysis of what the text says explicitly as well as inferences drawn from the text.

CCSS RL 11-12.1 Cite strong and thorough textual evidence to support analysis of what the text says explicitly as well as inferences drawn from the text, including determining where the text leaves matters uncertain.

Notes:

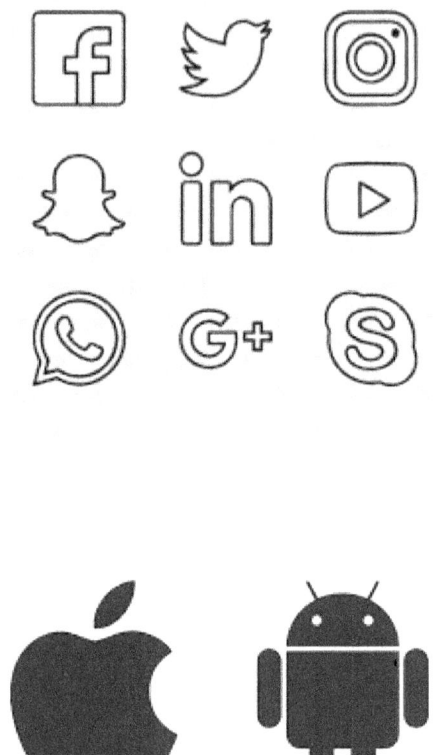

"Time is the one thing we all get the same amount of, (24 hours in a day) yet how we choose to use it will, forever determine the trajectory of our lives. Don't Waste your time, Invest your time..."

- Alan Gaines

Chapter 6
Social Media Is Killing Your Potential
"Where Did Time Go?"

Fam, keep it 💯... Do you know what the answer to "What is 9 + 10?" What do you say to someone with messed up shoes on? Finish this sentence… "Caash me outside, _____" If you answered; 21, What are those! And "How bout dat…" You can say that you are in with popular culture and the wave of internet sensations. I know, lots of that stuff you hear about in class. No, it is not a crime that you know these things. But if you are being real with yourself, you are a spending or should I say wasting, too much time on social media. Ok, lets go here first before we get into how you are wasting time.

How many of you want to be great? I know what you are saying to yourself, great at what? Ok, that's the point I want to get you to by the end of the book. For now, I will go to where you are and ask a different question. "How many of you want to make millions one day?" Alright, now we are on the same page. I know the majority of you said, "I Do".
Does this sound familiar? It should, we all have heard it. It's the words that are said at the end of a wedding ceremony. Which begins a new life of commitment to another individual for the rest of your life. Well, since I know that you more than likely said "I Do" to the question of Do you want to make millions? Then my question becomes, What is you level of commitment to making these millions become a reality?

Before we go any further lets get something straight. If you have a job or even in a lot of cases, a career, you don't <u>make</u> money, you get<u> paid</u> money. Let's clear this up, if you're working for someone else and not in total control, you are getting <u>paid</u>, you are not <u>making</u> money. (Hold up, didn't this chapter say something about social media? Why are we talking about jobs and money? - Don't trip. I got you, just stay with me alright?) Bottom line, if someone else is determining how much you get paid, even if you are negotiating a contract, you are not making money, you are getting paid. So, what is making money… Making money is when you create avenues for yourself to have multiple sources of income, most of which have no limit to how much money you can and will earn.

Ok, here is an example, let's take Drake. Of course he has a record deal and is locked into a percentage of that contract from that deal. That is what he gets paid. However, when Drake goes on tour, writes a song for someone, endorses Sprite or the Toronto Raptors, he is making money. The difference is, he is using his talent, image and ability to generate other sources of income and there is no limit on how much he can make from endorsements, because he can endorse as many products as he chooses as long as he makes himself available to those who want to use him to market their product. Now that you are beginning to see my point, let me answer your question, What does this have to do with me and social media? Well ask yourself, do you want to make money like Drake? You don't have to like him, or have the ability to rap. Would you take his bank account? I thought so… Ok, so what is the one thing interfering the most with your "I Do"? In other words, what is the one thing you could spend less time doing and use that time working on whatever you re going to do to make your millions?

LOL - I heard somebody saying, "School" - "It feels like a waste of time… I don't see the point!" - I feel where you are coming from and there maybe some truth to that, school is a necessary evil though, just keeping it 💯. (We already talked about school in Chapter 3 - Find your passion remember….) Back to the point, if you are being real with yourself than the answer is Social Media. I know you are thinking "Hold up, hold up - Drake is on twitter, snapchat & Instagram - so what are you talking about?" It's true, he is. However, Drake, like many other greats that you see, grew up before this social media era and when he was becoming Drake, he was not using his time tweeting or posting on social media. He was grinding, <u>period</u>. What does LeBron do come playoff time… Zero Dark Thirty - Unplugs from Social Media to chase his goal. Take notes from the greats…

Remember <u>You</u> said that <u>You</u> wanted to Make Millions… There is a universal law that input equals output. What are you inputting towards your millions? I'm sorry but, You can't wish your way to success. You are going to have to work for it. I know that you may have heard about this book or even got it from social media. Not to appear hypocritical, I said spend less time with social media, not get off of it completely. At one point I was giving this book away on Social Media, that is because I know that I had to go to the one place that I could find you… *On Social Media.*

Ask yourself, why do you have an Instagram, Snapchat or Twitter account? As you scramble to find the reason, remember - Society trains us to accept and never to question. More than likely, you have one because everyone else has one. Is there something wrong with that? Uhh sorta kinda it is… Let me give you a jewel that I would always give my students about time.

TIME IS THE ONE THING THAT EVERYONE GETS THE SAME AMOUNT OF BUT HOW WE USE OUR TIME IS WHAT MAKES ALL THE DIFFERENCE.

Time can be used in 3 ways - Investing / Spending / Wasting. If you invest your time now, you can spend your time how you desire when you get to that place that you want to be in life. However, if you waste your time it is highly unlikely that you will be able to spend your time as an adult doing things that you want to do. Too much time is being wasted on Social Media.

I am not trying to say that what you are doing is wrong, because, I know it that "It Goes Down in the DM". What I am saying is, we should evaluate our priorities and anything that is not going to help you get to what you want out of life, needs to be adjusted in regards to how much time you spend on or with it.

My point is we have this Narrative that watching YouTube, posting or retweeting things we think are funny, going live, taking 30 selfies to get the right one, looking at fights on WorldStar, etc… Is what we should do or be into, why? Everyone else is doing it and no one wants to be left out. You will never get 5 if you keep adding 2+2. Remember, input equals output. How much money have you made watching those videos? How many tests have you done just okay on, when you could have done better had you spent less time, "Doing it for the vine"? I know the answer is that you have not made any money and probably a lot of test you could have done better on. I hope it is becoming clear that social media is not the best way to invest your time.

It's actually a waste of time if you are not marketing a product or using it as a way to expose your skills and abilities to the world. If you are not producing respectable videos that are exposing your talents and abilities for the purpose of making your life better. Then please let me suggest that you switch some things up. Call it what you want, but I asked you if you wanted to make millions. If you can tell me how constantly wasting time on social media is going to help you get to where you want to be then keep doing what you are doing. If not please Reject the Narrative or as my brother Sherray would say, "It's ok to color outside the lines, broken crayons color too…" It is your picture.

The Big Picture

I remember having a conversation with my oldest daughter Assata in which I told her that Social Media is going to be the death of true greatness. Now that may not actually be, however, I do think it poses a huge threat to people truly reaching great heights. If you look at the people who have made it to the top of their profession and entered legendary status you always hear of them putting in countless hours at their craft. Whether it is Misty Copeland who got up in the early morning and practiced her dance in the motel room she lived in with her family. Steph Curry and how he would stay out all night working to perfect his jump shot that he had to change because of its bad form which is now picture perfect. Or Prince and how he would keep the neighborhood up playing music all day and night. Serena and Venus Williams learning to play tennis and the training their Dad put them through. Magic Johnson would go shovel the snow off of the basketball court near his home so he could practice before school.

I could go on and on but the point I making is that when you want something in life you are going to have to put in more time than you have ever imagined in order to make it a reality and spending that time on Social Media can and probably will cost you in the long run. Remember "I Do" means that you must put in a commitment. Input Equals Output… Put down the phone and put in the work…

Chapter 6
Discussion Questions

1.) <u>D.O.K. 1 Recall</u> How many hours per day do you spend on Social Media? How many hours per day do you spend with your talent or gift?

2.) <u>D.O.K. 1 Recall</u> Write out your typical day hour by hour. What can you do less of each day in exhcange for more time with your talent or gift?

3.) <u>D.O.K. 2 Analyze</u> Do you think the way you are currently spending your time will lead you to the path of success?

4.) <u>D.O.K. 4 Apply</u> What are positive ways in which you could use Social Media that wouldn't be considered a waste of time?

5.) <u>D.O.K. 4 Create</u> Create a schedule for your weekday that can allow you to be more productive.

Common Core Standards

CCSS R.I. 8.2 Analyze how a text makes connections among and distinctions between individuals, ideas, or events (e.g., through comparisons, analogies, or categories).

CCSS R.I. 9 - 10.2 Determine a central idea of a text and analyze its development over the course of the text, including how it emerges and is shaped and refined by specific details; provide an objective summary of the text.

CCSS 11 - 12.2 Determine two or more central ideas of a text and analyze their development over the course of the text, including how they interact and build on one another to provide a complex analysis; provide an objective summary of the text.

Notes:

This is probably My favorite picture because it symbolizes how giving time to young people manifest into greatness. Kadafi, Tavares, Mr. Gaines and DeAndre. 5th Grade Top 8th Grade Bottom.

My 2017 Offensive Lineman at Paramount High School

My Gary Steeler Pop Warner Jr. Midget State Champs

Some of the males from my 1st class on their graduation day. From Left, Tavion, Mr. Cherry, Lonnie, Sharod, DaJuan, Andre, AJ, Mr. Gaines and Coach Hicks.

Playing The Role...

Section 3:

How Conforming To Society's Narratives Can Derail Your Path To Success...

"Gang Bangin' ain't a lifestyle, it's a death style..."
— Cle 'Bone' Sloan

Whatever is the reason that people join gangs, the bottom line is the environment that surrouds being a part of a gang always involves being in some form of trouble with the law. Think wisely about the choices and decisions associated with being a member of something that has no long term benefits to your well being. While a gang may provide the comfort and security that your life feels it needs in the present moment, remember highly successful people always begin with the end in mind. What is the end game of being a part of or being affiliated with a gang?

-Alan Gaines

Chapter 7
Being A Gangster / Thug Is Cool

Look, I ain't ever been into any gang activity, but I know that some of you think that it is cool and you gotta be hard. When I was growing up, my hometown of Gary, Indiana earned the title of the "Murder Capital of America." My older brother lost his best friend when he was in the 6th grade because someone shot him in the chest over jokes. I knew then, that people don't regard the value of life the way that I do. I was blessed that my parents kept me away from that life. With that being said, in order to make this point I want to tell you a story from someone else's point of view, a Mother… Meet Mrs. Brantley:

Mrs. Brantley sits alone with her photo album, laptop and her box of tissue on the couch. The TV is on but it is only providing light to the room. She is deeply crying over these pictures. She is looking at photos of her son, Thomas, when he was a little boy. For the life of her, she can't figure out when, when was the moment her sweet little boy decided that what her and her husband provided him, wasn't enough. In her mind, they had done everything right. Mrs. Brantley refuses to believe that earlier today she was in a courtroom and heard that her only son, just 2 months from his 18th birthday will spend the next four years in prison for being an accessory to an armed robbery and assault. The pain in her chest and the migraine headache that was induced (brought upon) by stress has her unable to get any sleep. This is a dream she thinks to herself, no a 'nightmare'. This cannot be her life – this cannot be what has become of her precious child.

You see, Thomas was a rarity in the hood, he came from a two parent home and both his mom and his dad were college educated. (Not as rare as one would think though - this is the case more than a lot of people recognize) – Mrs. Brantley is a self employed business woman who is active in various community organizations and works with local politicians tirelessly to help make things better in their city. Mr. Brantley is an accountant at a large downtown firm and gets paid big money as a reward for the long hours he puts in, on what seems like at least 4 nights a week.

Thomas never had to want for much of anything, his parents always had enough and could afford to put him and his older sister, who is now 20 and a Junior in college, in the finest brand named clothing. Mrs. Brantley made sure that Thomas stayed fresh, he always had a really nice shoe game and always wore nice new clothes, rarely having to repeat outfits at school because he had a closet full of gear. His Dad made sure that he stayed with a fresh haircut, he kept the deep 360 waves. They went to the barber shop every other Saturday up until a few years ago when Thomas began high school.

On the surface everything appeared to be great, Mr. and Mrs. Brantley had provided everything that Thomas would need and he should be on the right path to what life tells us is success…

As Mrs. Brantley looks at the pictures, she notices a little less of a smile on his face in the pictures of Thomas in middle school. Looking hard at the pictures in the album she can see a little pain on her babies caramel complexion face– she thinks to herself, "Is this where it all begin to go wrong with Thomas?" Thomas always smiled as a kid, he was always tall for his age and loved to joke and play. Mrs. Brantley, feels a little guilty because this picture is from 7th grade, his first year in public school. In this particular picture, the smile that used to warm her heart isn't as wide as she had been so used to seeing.

Thomas had been in private school from kindergarten and the cost of tuition was getting to be a bit much for his parents and they decided that, since they had given Thomas a solid educational foundation, he would be fine at a public school. As his Pops put it, "He needs to be around his people, it will do him good. Maybe even toughen him up a bit." – Man did those words come back to haunt him.

You see in 7th grade, when Thomas got to his new school, things were different, A LOT DIFFERENT. This was the 1st time in his life he pulls out his homework and he is one of the few people in the class who has it done. At first he thinks nothing of it, but as time goes on he sees this theme repeating itself.

Remember those fresh clothes he wears? Well, that has all the little girls attention and some of his classmates and the older 8th grade boys started those hating whispers. Thomas is in class answering all the questions because for the most part the stuff the teacher is teaching, he went over last year if not the year before that! Thomas was thinking: "Oh, this is the life! The girls are jocking me and the teachers love me" – he was super in love with his new school…. For the 1st two months.

Those 8th grade boys who I mentioned and even some of the other 7th grade boys don't like that this "new kid" has came in and been getting all this attention. Thomas is confused because he is just being himself. One day at recess – while playing basketball – he noticed that he is the only one getting hard fouls and for the most part everyone even a few of his teammates are being mean to him. In his mind this is what his Dad probably means by toughening up…

As the year goes on things get worse, the name calling and bullying has started so – Thomas begins to clap back, being that Thomas was smart, he knew how to roast pretty well. What he didn't have was street smarts though, so one day the roasting turned serious and after class Thomas, being naïve, (unaware) - thought it was over. It wasn't, when he was walking down the hallway, a kid trips him as they are going around the corner and when he falls, the kid and about 4 other guys get to punching and kicking him and then run off. Thomas gets up and chases one of the kids and pushes him down. As usually the case, the teacher who happens to be in the hallway only sees Thomas' retaliation and it is reported as a fight. Mr. and Mrs. Brantley is upset with Thomas because he has never been in a fight but this comes along with the territory of a public school in their mind so no big deal. However, Thomas is on punishment at home, because *"We don't send you to school to fight."* Thomas tries to explain his case but both his Mom and Dad – don't want to hear it – *"No fighting, period*!" His punishment, no cell phone or video games for the next month. Thomas was the victim in this situation at school and at home he is being treated like the criminal! Thomas is hot – his parents don't want to listen and he has begun to hate the school.

The bullying of Thomas went on regularly through the rest of his 8th grade year as well. Thomas just grinned and bared it though because – in his mind his parents weren't going to listen anyway and even if he did tell them – they would just find a way to make what was happening his fault – he was tired of that and so he just kept it in.

By now Mrs. Brantley, is looking at Thomas's FaceBook page and as she is scrolling through his photos, she sees the pictures from 9th grade. The year that she begin to no longer notice her child. Thomas is now calling himself TB and he has all types of pics with his middle finger up posted on FaceBook. Looking at the pictures Mrs. Brantley is confused because through the tears streaming down her face she is wondering is the middle finger that her baby has up directed at her?

This pain she is feeling is sooo deep, her mind is racing with horrifying thoughts. Her baby is going to be locked up with men twice and three times his size and age. She cries, thinking, "Are they going to rape my baby? Are they going to beat my baby up? He can't fight, how is he going to defend himself? She lets out a scream! It's 2 am in the morning and she just doesn't get it? WHAT HAPPENED? WHY? GOD WHY? What did we do wrong, what could we have done different?"

As she looks at these pictures of TB, because this definitely is not Thomas, she thinks, "Was it the music? We gave him a phone and let him listen to whatever he wanted as long as he kept good grades…" Which was the case until late in his freshman year. These pictures she is scrolling through may as well be carbon copies of a Chicago Drill Music Video… Shirts wraped around his face, pants sagging, boxers showing, the Louie' Belt she bought him and he is throwing up some gang sign she doesn't recognize with his hands. Mrs. Brantley looks harder, trying to find the little boy that would spend hours with his Dad on the weekend building model cars and racing remote control cars in the big parking lot up the street. "Lord why is my son going to spend the next 4 years of his life in prison, Lord WHY?!"

She thinks back to that time when he was in the 10th grade, in which she realized that the money from her purse was missing… She knew he had stolen the money because when he asked her for $20 two days before, she said no and he got really upset and wouldn't talk to her for the rest of the day. She went to go put some gas in the car and noticed the $20 bill missing from her purse. She wanted so bad to tell his father but the night before Thomas and Mr. Brantley had gotten into a huge argument that turned physical over Thomas coming in the house smelling like weed and his eyes were bloodshot red. On top of a progress report with 4 C's and 2 D's. Grades that Thomas had never gotten in his life.

Mrs. Brantley is playing back the end of that argument between him and his Dad – which ended with Thomas telling his Dad that he doesn't care anymore and that his Dad should, as Thomas put it "Go back to work, that's all you do anyway. You don't ever have time for me no more so don't worry about my life! Go do your job." This hurt Mr. Brantley's pride and everyone in the house knew it. There was a lot of truth in what Thomas was saying. Mr. Brantley was spending more and more time at work, doing more and more to get that promotion and spending less time with Thomas. You see like most parents, Mr. Brantley thought that as his children got older, they could spend less time with them, when in fact that is the opposite of what a child truly needs. The older a child gets the more they will need their parents, because its during this time that they have the most questions and need the most direction.

Mrs. Brantley stares at the screen and sees it! TB made a post on instagram of him and her the Tuesday before he got arrested with his boys the Saturday of that same week. The post was a selfie of him and her eating breakfast that morning, they were two weeks into the summer vacation going into his senior year and the two of them were just hanging out. She woke up that morning feeling good, she had things to do at her office and a couple of errands to run, but she thought, not today… I am going to make Thomas breakfast and ask him to sit and watch Black-ish on the Firestick. That was their show and they needed to catch up. So she got up and made his favorite, pancakes and eggs. She called to the room, "Thomas how many pancakes do you want?" His reply, "3 please" he still hadn't loss his manners. She continues cooking as Thomas, now all of 6'4" with a slender yet muscular physique, comes out of the room with his model car magazine.

Mrs. Brantley looks up from the pot noticing him walking toward the kitchen. She wants to mention something about his hair, which is in a perfectly lined yet nappy Fro – Hawk. Mrs. Brantley wishes he would cut it and go back to the nice 360 waves he had as a kid. However, she knows that she didn't put off the things she had to do today to start an argument with her son that she knows she desperately needs to reach. So she just looks back down in the pot and keeps her comments to herself. By now, Thomas has made it to the kitchen and says with a smile, "Good Morning Ma" to which she replied "Good Morning TB" in an attempt to relate and his respect his wishes. He never let's anyone call him Thomas anymore. So Mrs. Brantley was shocked when he told her, "It's cool Ma, you can call me Thomas." To this news she gave more than a raised eyebrow, she almost dropped all the pancakes in amazement. Mrs. Brantley replied "Whoa – what has gotten into you today? Is it that I am cooking pancakes? Because I can make pancakes everyday if this is going to be your reaction!" Thomas laughs it off – "Nawl Ma, I just miss… us" Mrs. Brantley is puzzled and says, "Miss us?! Boy, me and your daddy ain't went nowhere! What you talking about miss us?" Thomas straightens up: "Ma you know what I mean, I miss how things were, we used to be a family, Ma – before Shelly went off to college and Daddy wasn't working crazy hours… We used to eat every night together, now my food be on the stove or you calling me to see what I want to eat on your way home… I just miss the way things were for us – you know what I am talking about."

Mrs. Brantley begins tearing up as she is looking at Thomas dressed like TB… She hears him, she hadn't heard "his" voice in so long that she couldn't help but cry and because something was telling her to channel that emotion – she grabbed her cell phone after she finished hugging him so tightly and crying. She said "Oooh let me take a picture of this" Thomas put down his fork and leaned in next to his mother and gave a really big smile as she snapped the picture. "Ma send me that picture, I like that one" – she doesn't hesitate and sends him the pic. Mrs. Brantley turns to Thomas and says, "Baby, I know things are different, and I miss them too… Trust me, probably more than you do and me and your Daddy know that it is our fault, we just trying to make things better and get more for ourselves. Shelly's tuition isn't cheap and that is why your Daddy been working so late – heck you going to be going off to school soon – I know that your grades have slipped a bit but you can pull them back up – you always been really smart." Thomas is tearing up just a little now and respectfully cuts her off:

"Ma I know that but, its not like it was, we were a family and I miss that. Like for real miss that. I bet Dad don't even remember the last time we went to race our remote control cars. We used to go up to the lot, while you and Shelly would go shopping. We would meet up and get something to eat or go see a movie. Now, it's like nothing, don't nobody do nothing – Ma. So that's why I be kicking it with the Bros – I mean, I know they not the best dudes to be around but they look out for me, they treat me like family. They always around when I am going through things, they make me feel like I belong Ma. I mean I know they not the best, I know it, but it's better than being around here doing nothing."

Mrs. Brantley looks at Thomas and just hugs him again. She feels that breakthrough that she had been praying about coming, she senses that Thomas no longer wants to be apart of hanging with his Bros and just wants things to be like they were. So she makes Thomas a promise,"This Saturday your sister will be back in town for the weekend and we were going to hang out – I'll tell your Dad that you two need to hang out and he could take you to the auto show at convention center – and later that night we will all go to a movie okay? How does that sound?" Thomas is finishing his breakfast and a deep smile is coming over his face, "That sounds good Ma." They finished eating and binged watched about 8 episodes of Black-ish.

Three days later, Thomas is sitting in his room listening to Tidal when, his boy D calls him around 10:30 at night and said "Let's go kick it at Lil Man house"– TB is thinking about his plans with his family the next day and pauses for a moment. "Cool, I'll roll but I got something to do early tomorrow so I gotta get back aight", D said "Fa sho fam – I got you – I'll drop you off myself – finna come grab you so throw some clothes on bro, see you in about 15 minutes." About 45 minutes later, TB gets the text that D is outside, he grabs his hat and keys. He walks to his parents closed door and yells – "I'll be right back!" to which Mrs. Brantley says puzzled, "Where you going?" TB says – "With D to Lil' Man house real fast" Mrs. Brantley had an uneasy feeling but her conversation on Tuesday and their plans tomorrow made her feel a little better about it – so she replied – "Don't forget about our plans for tomorrow" TB replies "I won't, I am coming right back, D just want me to roll with him" he hears Mrs. Brantley's voice – "OK – Be Safe" – TB starts to the door and then stops – he goes back to the door and Thomas says – "Mom, Dad I love y'all" he doesn't wait for a reply – he just hurries to the car and hops in.

The car smells like bud, which he is used to but Thomas thought it was only going to be D in the car. Nope, Rell and Marc are with him and TB sits in the back a little more reserved than usual. Thomas knows that Rell and Marc aren't really the type of guys he likes to be around. They legit be on slanging drugs and playing stick up kid in the streets. Marc is 19 and Rell is 18, D is 17, only a few months older than Thomas who was about to turn 17. Marc is D's older cousin and D holds drugs for him sometimes because he is also the weed man. Marc stay strapped with a gun on him at all times. Thomas knows this and is feeling a little weird. Thomas wants to tell D to just take him back home because he don't like being in a car with Marc and Rell. But he promised his boy that he would roll with him and he doesn't want to make them feel like he weak or too scary to be around them. Thomas he is thinking of a way to get out of the car… He texted his sister Shelley – CALL ME AND SOUND PANIC'D – SAY I NEED TO COME HOME RIGHT NOW – DON'T ASK JUST DO IT – Too bad, Shelly has passed out for the night, her drive back home from college for the weekend has caught up to her… The text message goes unread.

Thomas is sitting waiting for the call, Marc is right next to him in the back seat and he begins to start rolling a blunt. Marc's gun is digging in his waist and he pulls it out, puts the safety on and tells Thomas "Here, hold this while I roll up." Thomas is like, "Cool." He puts the gun on his lap and sits back – he looks at his phone, hoping his sister hurries up and calls him – no call – he is thinking to himself "Come on Shell." He looks out his window impatiently, as the car pulls up to the light.

At the light across from them is a cop car – he notices it and thinks to himself – "Aww Sh.." He starts praying, "Lord, please don't let these cops turn around and get behind us." The light flashes green and D takes off cautiously, just not too slow to be noticeable. Yep, you guessed it, the cop car does a U turn and gets behind them. Thomas is thinking "F#$&! I am about to go to jail over some weed!"

Thomas had no idea that two hours earlier, all three of them had robbed a couple coming out a strip mall for some jewelry and cash. So the cops run plates and put the lights on and spotlight in the car. D yells, "Bro should I try to lose them?" Thomas is thinking *For What*, he yells out, "Hell No!" D is like "You right, you right… When I stop we gone all run?!"

Thomas is still lost… D slowly pulls over and stops the car. Immediately, Rell, Marc and D – take off – Thomas follows the officers orders and puts hands out the car – one officer takes off after them running. The other officer comes to the car where Thomas is sitting and "Yells don't move!" when he gets to the window – Thomas still has both hands out of the window, the officer yells – "Is that your firearm?" Thomas is thinking "What firearm?" He looks down and the .45 that Marc handed him is still sitting on his lap under his cell phone… He knows it is all over…

Two hours later Mrs. Brantley got the call from Lake County Correctional Facility and the news that Thomas was being held on 1 million dollar bail for his role in an armed robbery. Hearing what she could only hope was a dream, Mrs. Brantley let's out a painful scream. The sound startles Shelley who hops out of bed and runs to her parents' room to see what was going on. "Ma! What's wrong?! Are you okay!" By this time her Dad is asking the same question, tears are rolling uncontrollably down Mrs. Brantley's face as she has come to the pause in her cry. Mrs. Brantley is trying to gather herself to tell them that Thomas has been arrested. The news hits Shelley like a ton of bricks, she slowly goes over to the bed and lays her weeping (crying) head on her Dad's shoulder as he hugs his wife. In disbelief Shelly goes back to her room and sits on her bed trying to put her thoughts back together. Through the tears she sees her phone is lighting up from a missed text message, she grabs the phone and sees the message from Thomas… Her heart sinks and the tears begin to flow even faster… She may never forgive herself for missing that text…

I wrote this chapter from a Mothers perspective, because lots of times fellas we get so wrapped up in ourselves that we forget who else can be effected by our actions. I know that Thomas maybe a lot different from you, however, it doesn't have to be crime that you are into that makes your mother suffer. It could be your grades, it could be your behavior, it could many things. We have to Reject The Narrative that a gang or your bros is family… Your FAMILY is YOUR FAMILY. They may be cool and they may be there for you and make you feel like family. However, true family are the people who want what is best for you and will not try to get you to do things that you know are not right. I know they cool but you gotta Flip The Script. They have accepted their Narrative and feel that they can't do any better, so that is why they try to keep you around.

It may not seem this way but people with no ambition or goals often try to make others around them have the same outlook on life. Therefore you must be careful who you hang with because before you know it you can find yourself in a situation like Thomas. Thomas was full of promise yet his life has been derailed because of poor choices of friends. I once heard, sparrows flock, eagles don't… They fly by themselves. Be an eagle… Think about your Moms, or your Grandmoms, do you want her going through what Mrs. Brantley had to deal with? His family, may not have had time for him, but that doesn't mean that they stopped loving him. Think about all the people who love you. How do you think what you are doing, is making them feel right now? Flip The Script. Put your real family 1st!

The BIG PICTURE

Playing the role of a Thug or Gangster isn't cool. I am not going to spend time lecturing you about how trying to be in the streets, has two outcomes, being dead or in jail. Why, because we all know that, what I will say is, think about the people in your life that love you. No one who truly loves you, wants to see you harmed in any fashion. It's dangerous enough being young and black in America, I mean look at what happened to Trayvon Martin, Tamir Rice and a long list of other young men who have been killed over nothing. And they were not in the streets.

Your life is not valued by society at large, so nothing can be more important than the value that you place on yourself. I will say that again…

NOTHING CAN BE MORE IMPORTANT THAN THE VALUE THAT YOU PLACE ON YOURSELF!!!

I know living in the hood, if that is where you stay, seeing crackheads, prostitutes, murders, abandoned buildings, drugs and every other thing that you have been exposed to makes it very hard to feel that God has more than this in store for you. I get it, I grew up in Gary, Indiana in the 80's and 90's – I survived seeing the same things going on around me. I had the chance to get into all the wrong things, however, I made a decision that I wanted more and I worked until I got it. The point is this…

CHOOSE LIFE!

It's sad that in 2017 Black people still have to march and rally to let the world know that Black Lives Matter. We have to do more than just talk about how we matter; it starts with you youngsters valuing yourself and your life. When we start to love ourselves and think about others we are affecting with things we do in this gang lifestyle – we will show the world that Black Lives Do Matter – because we are no longer killing each other or innocent people for nothing. Real Talk, let's make our mothers cry tears of joy – no more tears of pain!

Chapter 7
Discussion Questions

1.) <u>D.O.K. 2 Explain</u> Have you ever been in a situation in which your parents didn't listen to you? Describe how it made you feel?

2.) <u>D.O.K. 3 Evaluate</u> Describe the difference between Thomas in 7th and 10th grade?

3.) <u>D.O.K. 2 Evaluate</u> How does the Brantley family no longer spending time together impact Thomas?

4.) <u>D.O.K. 3 Evaluate</u> Why does the author say that "Thomas" tells his parents "Mom, Dad I love y'all" but "TB" gets in the car with "D"? Why do you think the author made this distinction between being in the home and outside the house?

5.) <u>D.O.K. 4 Create</u> If you were Thomas and you saw Marc & Rell, in the car would you have told D that you didn't want to ride? Why or why not? What would be an influence on your decision?

Common Core Standards

CCSS RL 8.3 Analyze how particular lines of dialogue or incidents in a story or drama propel the action, reveal aspects of a character, or provoke a decision.

CCSS RL 9 - 10.3 Analyze how complex characters (e.g., those with multiple or conflicting motivations) develop over the course of a text, interact with other characters, and advance the plot or develop the theme.

CCSS RL 11 - 12.3 Analyze the impact of the author's choices regarding how to develop and relate elements of a story or drama (e.g., where a story is set, how the action is ordered, how the characters are introduced and developed).

Notes:

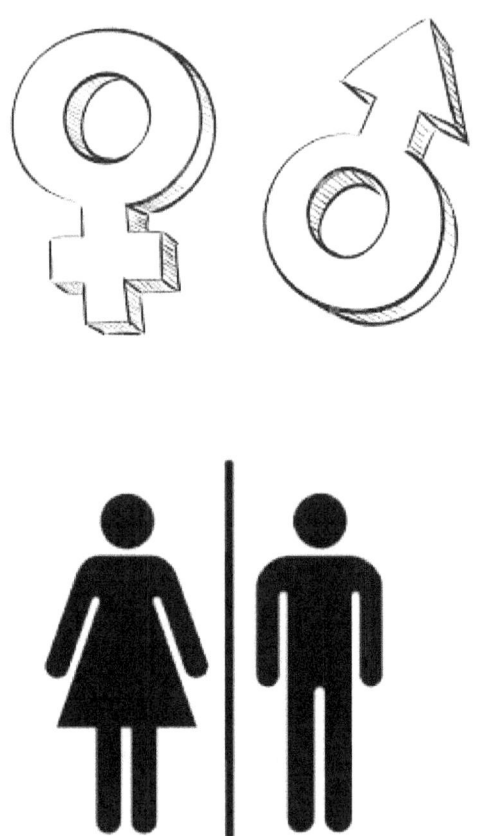

"I Always Told The Young Men That I Mentored And Taught, To Treat The Young Ladies Like They Wanted Someone To Treat Their Mother, Because Some Day These Young Ladies Will Be Someones Mother."

- Alan Gaines

Chapter 8
How Many Bodies You Got?
The Narrative & Womanizing

I wonder why we take from our women / Why we rape our women / Do We Hate Our Women?
I think it is time to kill for our women / Time to heal our women / Be real to our women / Cuz if we don't we'll have a race of babies / That hate the Ladies /That Make Our Babies…"

Keep Your Head Up - TuPac

Pac definitely said it better than I could have. So I felt this Chapter should start with the words of someone who everyone could relate too. I personally feel that this Narrative may be the most detrimental to our community because in my opinion, more people are affected by the results of this Narrative than any other.

My Introduction to the Womanizing Narrative

I honestly cannot remember when I got the Narrative that being a man meant being a player, pimp or ladies man. I cannot remember or put a finger on my introduction of the idea and notion that women are to be objectified. The crazy thing about this is that most men probably can't remember their first encounter with it either. Here is an instance that I vividly remember from my childhood.

I remember going over my Uncle Aaron's house one day. My older brother Sherray brought his girlfriend. Now, before I go any further, yes, Uncle Aaron, was "That Uncle". My brother had to be no more than 16, which put me around 12 years old. As usually the case, we came in the backdoor and my Uncle Aaron , my Uncle Johnny and two of my Uncle's friends are all in the kitchen playing cards. Sherray and his girlfriend were in front of me and my mother was in front of them. So as we are going into the house my Uncle yells, BILLY BOOTY!!! (a nickname he gave my brother - he has a big butt). Sherray knew what was coming because this was the type of house my Uncle ran.

Sherray gives a nervous laugh and says "Wsup, Uncle A?" My Uncle said, "Dang boy, what you and that pretty girl been doing? You got hair all over your face, I know you been doing something?!" Mind you, he has been in the house a cool 2 minutes before my Uncle is going in. Before Sherray could answer, my Uncle turns to the young lady and says "Girl are you giving my nephew some?" Yep no filter, Uncle A went hard…

Looking back on it over 20 years later, this was horrible and I can only imagine what the young lady had to be thinking or feeling. Besides all of the obvious disrespect that is wrong with the situation. My Uncle Aaron was practically the family Patriarch, or key male figure for one side of the family. Everybody was always at my Uncle Aarons house and parts of his personality were so loving and endearing that many people wanted to be around him. I don't want you to think that my Uncle was some horrible person, he would and did give plenty of people the shirt off of his back. He was loved by the community and at one point a key figure in local politics in my hometown. This is also what made his actions in my opinion okay at the time. I looked up to my Uncle Aaron because he had so much respect and love from people all over the city. So not until I got much older did I ever think that his thinking was wrong. It clearly is wrong, women should not be mistreated or viewed as sexual objects.

Womanizing in Our Society

As young men, we are so impressionable and the people we look up to a lot of the times are the ones who pass us Narratives that we never stop to question. As it relates to women or girls, you don't have to go beyond that cell phone in your pocket to get a Narrative that tells you that women are objects that are to be used. I get the feeling that you don't fully get what I am saying.

Ok, so look at it like this, the majority of the women you see in videos, especially ones in which the male is the artist, has on more articles of clothes than the amount of words you hear them say. Putting it plainly, the women you see in the videos have little to no clothes on, are probably twerking or doing something else that promotes sex and they probably never speak in the video. I will say that again… THEY PROBABLY NEVER SPEAK IN THE VIDEO.

So, what is being said to you is that a women should be used to make you think about sex, not voice their opinion or themselves. That is just a little something to think about next time you go on YouTube or watch some music video. My point is that from a very young age, the world is telling you that women are symbols of sex and are to be manipulated and used for that purpose.

This is not an idea that you will ever escape. American businesses make billions off of the idea that sex sells and will continue to make that a huge part of society. What I want you to understand is that, this idea is something that is being given to you and is not natural. This idea of manipulating and basically pimping women is not right and you know it, because you would not want to see your mother, grandmother or sister used or mistreated.

I want you to understand that all messages are double sided. If society is telling you that is okay to objectify and sexualize women. Then it is also telling you that it is okay for you to be the one who objectifies and sexualizes women. Let me be the one who tells you - THIS IS NOT OKAY! Oprah said it best in her Golden Globes speech… TIMES UP! A thought that Pac tried to relay when he says Time to heal our women, be real to our women…

I know that you are probably thinking that you don't see any broken or damaged girls who need healing. Well, let's take you mind back to Chapter 1, when we were talking about the "other" girl that you used to make sure your boys couldn't keep clowning you…

A Walk In A Females Shoes...

Let's call her Diamond. Why? Because our Black girls are all precious, priceless jewels that are made from intense pressure. Like a Diamond, they must be mined from the dirty of society and properly shaped in order for the world to admire their beauty…

Diamond was blessed with a beautiful dark complexion and a gorgeous smile. She is truly beautiful, yet she doesn't see this when she looks in the mirror. Inside, she knows that she is pretty, but after years and years of seeing other girls get all the attention from boys and hearing them talk about this girls and that girl, Diamond has gotten into the habit of staring in the mirror trying to look for the flaw that makes the boys look the other way when it comes to her and her beauty.

The sad part is, Diamond thinks that it is a physical feature that she doesn't possess that makes the boys look past her. When the truth is that it is her strength, confidence and strong will that makes boys pass over her. Boys look for weaknesses and flaws that they can exploit. Men look for strength and support that can be built upon. Diamond is not superficial, (into material things) she has self respect and wasn't the type to really put herself out there as easy. Boys didn't get the vibe from her that she is into things that they on the hunt for. Which is someone that y'all can get with physically. So while Diamond is in the mirror looking for what is wrong with her outside appearance, she will be much older before she realizes that it is what is on the inside that has kept her from the type of guys who are out to misuse her and will eventually attract the man that is destined to love her. Real men want strength and support as much as they want love and beauty. Unfortunately for Diamond, boys will surround her for the foreseeable future.

Diamond's Dad is gone just like yours maybe, so the lessons you not getting about how to be a man, she is not getting the lessons on how a man should treat a lady. Diamond is hurting and yearning for that same empty space that your pops left you with, to be fulfilled in her. This is where the problem lies. With no emotional connection from her father, Diamond feels internally like she has been rejected from the one man who should always be there to love her unconditionally, her Daddy. This is the perfect recipe for developing low self esteem and being manipulated.

There is an old saying that "Women raise their daughters and love their sons…" Which means, Mothers tend to be hard on their girls and take it easy on their sons. I have 3 daughters and 1 son, so I can say that I see this from time to time in my own home. Well Diamonds' Dad isn't around and her mother is raising her.

So as Diamond is getting about 16 or 17 and she isn't feeling the love neither at home or from the guys at her school, which begins to eat at and eventually destroyed that strong will and self respect. Consistently seeing what seems like all the other girls putting themselves out there for boys are getting the attention. Honestly, or how do y'all say it, TBH, Diamond doesn't want the physical things that boys are offering or that she sees the other girls getting from guys. Diamond just wants to sit on the phone and talk to a boy and laugh, joke and have a good time. In essence, Diamond just wants attention to help feel that void, left by her Dad and to help confirm a feeling that she holds deep down inside that she is, pretty. Diamond truly wants to be the person that a guy is into for who she is, not what she can do with or give to a guy.

It is this desire to be liked, to be loved, to be the center of someone's attention besides her own that eventually makes Diamond compromise her morals and self respect for that guy she is into, who just happens to be you.

Yep, you guessed it, you started flirting with her one day in class and the next thing you know you asked for her Instagram and little did you know, that was all it took. Diamond has been waiting for a guy to come along and give her some attention. You hit her up in the DM and it has been going down ever since. Diamond is no longer looking in the mirror trying to find that flaw because now someone finally sees her beauty. Her hopes are up and her feelings and emotions can't be held back anymore because it was you that noticed them. Diamond has started to change how she wears her clothes, she is showing a little more cleavage and has thrown a few skirts in her rotation. All of which you like and you don't hesitate to mention when y'all text. All the attention feels like prayers have been answered and Diamond is willing to do whatever you would like in order to keep that relationship that you started going.

That is why Diamond is willing to look past your girlfriend and play that SZA role, you know, the girl on "The Weekend". Diamonds' long awaited moment of being noticed has arrived and you were the one who did it. Beneath the surface, Diamond is damaged from the scars left by her Father and all the years she felt unpretty because she was passed up and passed over for girls that boys felt looked better or had more to offer. All this has created an individual who is willing to sacrifice herself physically in exchange for the comforts and emotional highs of being wanted in any fashion from a guy.

Take a second and tap back into your emotion and feelings of rejection because your Dad isn't around or just a time where you were told by the world that you were not good enough. You would have to intensify that by at least 10 or more to understand what a girl goes through if she doesn't have her Dad. Most males are fortunate enough to know the feeling of being loved by a woman because 9 times out of 10 you are likely to have your mother. There are tons of "Diamonds" out there who on the other hand will never have that luxury because they don't have their Father. Being that they don't know what it means to be loved by a man, they become vulnerable to be objectified and manipulated by one.

When you mix that with how you see our society treating women, Diamond has accepted this Narrative, that this is the way things are supposed to be and has now totally buried her strength and strong will to meet her need… The Need to be LOVED. Diamond looks around and she is seeing almost everyone doing adult things around her so she doesn't see the crime in her doing it too. In her mind if this means that she will get what she never got from her Dad or boys growing up, the attention and the feeling of love, she doesn't find this trade off to be so bad. In the end, the touching and kissing feels good, so although she would rather just hold hands or sit with you at lunch, she goes along with it because everyday she looks forward to the text, pics, and conversations. Finally, Diamond feels wanted.

Well, it wasn't so bad when you were into her, but now you find someway to tell her that you not dealing with her no more. Your girlfriend has found out about y'all relationship and you decide to be faithful to your girlfriend. Your intentions may never been to hurt her, but you were never into her for who she was, your intentions with her were all about you and your personal desires.

Unfortunately for Diamond, she did not see this coming and she doesn't see the reason that y'all can't continue talking and being friends. Diamond yearns for your friendship but you cut it off completely and she goes back to that mirror and now what she sees is completely unrecognizable. She no longer sees the beauty she once saw in herself and more importantly, she doesn't feel that strength that used to fill her up inside. That strength has been replaced with even lower self esteem. She can't think about anything but how low she had to be, to allow herself to think that you really liked her and wanted to be with her.

Diamond felt that once you got to know who Diamond is on the inside, that you would leave your girl and the two of you would be together. You may never have sold her that dream but this is how she envisioned things playing out. Diamond thought she finally had someone who gave her the assurance that she is worth being loved

The sad irony is that this scenario will play itself out more times with other guys because she is still looking to have that need of love fulfilled and she knows that she did nothing wrong. She simply chose the wrong guy. When you add in the fact that her Dad isn't there to show her the value of her worth from a man's point of view, Diamond is a broken winged butterfly that needs to be healed in order to catch the breeze beneath her wings and rise to the heights that she is destined to reach. To quote Pac again, "Time to heal our women / Be Real to our women."

In the words of School Boy Q - "That Part". The biggest problem in the situation is that we are not being real to our women. I am speaking to you from my own experience. There are women who I hurt as girls and young ladies because I had accepted this Narrative of being a Pimp or Player. I wasn't being real to women, I was using them for my own personal gratification and for that I am truly sorry. I was doing what I felt was an obligation in order to uphold a reputation that I had built. Truth be told, I did not have the maturity to consider the results of my actions on the girls and young ladies I was damaging in the process. I have prayed for forgiveness for my actions. I am simply trying to give you the power to create a New Narrative. That hurting girls for the purpose of being considered a player or pimp in the eyes of others is not cool, please stop.

If you are doing it, then deep down inside, you know that you are being fake, not real. That is why its called trying to "run game", because you are not being real with them. You are trying to get what you can and if that means lying then "Oh well". Its all about you and what she will give you so you can go brag to your boys. You are stepping on a lot of Diamonds, when real jewels should be handled with care.

One last note on Diamond. I want you to know that some "Diamonds" never get shaped and placed on showcase. Some scars never heal and she may possibly lead a broken life, with trust issues, insecurities and low self esteem. I am not saying that this is totally the boy who breaks her hearts' fault.

What I am saying is that we must begin to see the value in our women and in ourselves. I want you to understand why it is an absolute must, that we begin to see women as priceless jewels in our communities. Our women must be cherished and protected and not objectified and disrespected.

On a bigger note, we as men have to find a greater value in ourselves. When you are willing to do anything with anybody you begin to devalue who you are. Let's take a rapper who does a feature with just about any and everybody. I honestly can't keep up with who is out rapping today but I am sure that it is somebody that every time you turn on the radio, you hear this person rapping on this song and on that song. They might even be skilled, I am not saying that they not nice, but when you hear them on every song people tend to get tired of them. Same goes for you bro, stop trying to do a feature with any and everyone. The biggest and best artist you see don't over use themselves. Tupac didn't do a collaboration with every artist, neither did Biggie. Beyonce is not singing the hook on every song on the radio. Top tier artist are more exclusive. They limit their access which keeps the fans wanting more. Players get played out, when you are putting yourself out there eventually you going to gain a reputation that you get a round and at some point girls are going to look at you like damaged goods.

The BIG PICTURE
Flipping The Script On Womanizing

1. Treat women like you would want your mother to be treated. - I think this is very simple, you would not want anyone doing things and saying the stuff you may say or do to your Mom. Even if you are seeing it in your home… You know it is not right, remember these young ladies will be someone's mother one day.

2. Value YOURSELF - Not only are you disrespecting her, you are disrespecting yourself! My sister Shelley always told me "Everything Good To You, Ain't Good For You". There are all types of STD's out there. God said your body is a temple, it's time you start treating it like one.

3. Be Vocal about your stance to be respectful toward women - You may never know who your decision will influence. People are always watching, even if you are not the type that usually speaks up. The choices and decisions you make affect others. Be a leader, not a follower.

4. Be Real To Our Women! - I can appreciate a guy who will not date or mess around with a young lady because he respects her. If you know that you are not into the young lady - let her know. You may hurt her feelings but she will respect the truth more than being misused! Be Real To Our Women.

Chapter 8
Discussion Questions

1.) <u>D.O.K. 3 Analyze</u> How do the images in music videos influence what you think about women?

2.) <u>D.O.K. 2 Explain</u> How does Diamond's insecurities make her feel like she must compromise herself in order to get affection from a male?

3.) <u>D.O.K. 2 Evaluate</u> Explain how Diamond may feel when she is told she can't be friends with you? Have you ever played with a girls emotions? Why?

4.) <u>D.O.K. 3 Evaluate</u> Do you feel that guys who have a lot of girls are devaluing themselves? If you don't think so, why do you think society frowns upon a girl who deals with a variety of guys? Discuss the double standard?

5.) <u>D.O.K. 3 Evaluate</u> Why do you think society objectifies women? Would you be upset if someone treated your mother or daughter like you treat women? If so, what are some of the ways that you change your attitude and behavior towards women?

Common Core Standards

CCSS R.I. 8.2 Analyze how a text makes connections among and distinctions between individuals, ideas, or events (e.g., through comparisons, analogies, or categories).

CCSS R.I. 9 - 10.2 Determine a central idea of a text and analyze its development over the course of the text, including how it emerges and is shaped and refined by specific details; provide an objective summary of the text.

CCSS 11 - 12.2 Determine two or more central ideas of a text and analyze their development over the course of the text, including how they interact and build on one another to provide a complex analysis; provide an objective summary of the text.

Notes:

"We Are All Products of Our Environment. The Problem Is, That Now More Than Ever, Too Many Of Us Are Becoming A Victim Of Our Environment As Well."

- Alan Gaines

Chapter 9
Nobody Makes It From Here..
The Narrative and Where You From

They made light of / My type of / Dream seems dumb/ They said wise up /How many guys-a / You see making it from here? / The world don't like us /Is that not clear? / Alright but / I'm Different / I can't base what I'm gon' be /Offa what everybody isn't / They Don't listen... / Just whisperin' /
Behind my back / No vision / Lack of Ambition / So Whack!

So Ambitious - Jay Z

One of the biggest obstacles of being from the hood is that people can't see beyond their environment. To be very clear about what I am saying to you, people in your immediate surroundings, specifically, friends, (both your age and a little bit older) teachers, coaches, people in your neighborhood, sadly maybe even your parents, will tell you that what you are thinking or dreaming of one day becoming is an impossible idea or dream. What usually happens, because of their influence on you, we take their Narrative as our own. Since no one believes in you, you stop fighting and putting in the work towards the dreams you had your heart set on achieving. I can't even count how many times I have seen someone allow themselves to be talked out of reaching their goals. And every time it ended in that person leading a life of average and depression. I don't want you to be that person who accepts what others can't see. Let's dig deeper into what Jay Z is saying to you in this verse…

They made light of / my type of / Dream seems dumb / They said wise up / How many guys - a / you see makin' it from here...

In Chapter 3 I told you about my student Robert who got clowned for wanting to be a pastry chef, but he didn't let that break him. If we keep it 💯, we all probably like something that we are too embarrassed to tell other about because we know we would get clowned or roasted for if people knew about it.

Real talk though, just because people around you can't see what you are looking at, is no reason to stop going after your dreams. This is what Jay is saying with this verse - *They made light of* (to clown or roast). *My type of dream seems dumb* (being a photographer, an author, a meteorologist, a paleontologist, whatever you dream maybe) *How many guys-a / you see makin' it from here?* I am not sure where you live; Gary, Flynt, East St. Louis, Newark, Jackson, Chiraq, Fayettenam, South Central, Liberty City, etc... wherever you maybe from, the people who can't see your dream or goals will use your surroundings to convince you that, all the success in the world, which lives inside of you can not be reached because of where you live. And when you look around at the dope dealers, abandoned buildings, rundown schools, teenage mothers who got baby daddies who in his 20's, gunshots going off every night when you lay your head on your pillow at night…. It is very easy to believe what they are saying is true. Let me say this loudly…

THIS MAYBE YOUR REALITY - BUT THAT DOESN'T MEAN IT HAS TO BE YOUR DESTINY!!!

Your Destiny will be decided by the actions you make from this very moment in your life. Your Reality is what is currently in your life. Nothing more and nothing less.

<u>A Deeper Look Into Destiny Vs Reality</u>

Let's do this - I want everyone to think about your report card. I am going to show you how we are conditioned, or trained to think that what we have and where we are is what we are destined to be, which is not true. Ok, think about what a report card is and when you receive it. A report card is a graded reflection (showing) of what you did during the grading period. Most grading periods are 9 weeks, the report card is a reflection of how well you performed during those 9 weeks, nothing more nothing less. However, when we get a "bad" report card, we begin to feel dumb or stupid and in some cases we hear this same thing from our parents when we get the reports. This makes us begin to view ourselves in a negative way. We start to think we are dumb and stupid and that is why we become so defensive about someone calling us either dumb or stupid. It's why some of us either stop or never start asking questions in class. We are afraid that this is what people are going to think of us, we are stupid, because eventually we start to think this of ourselves. I'm just keeping it 💯!

The sad truth is - this is so far from your destiny. Staying on the report card - being that it is only a REFLECTION, of what you did during those 9 weeks! When we look over those 9 weeks and what happened during that time - it could have been a lot of different things. You could have moved, your parents could be going through a divorce, your sibling could be sick, your house could have caught on fire, you could be going through an emotional break up - you could have started a new job. The list can go on and on, you could have just been in a funk and flat out did not feel like doing any schoolwork! I am not making excuses, I am telling you that life happens and you know this. We must stop looking at how well we did on something as an indicator of what we will be in our future.

We are trained to feel that what we got and where we are determines who we are and what we will become. Whatever situation you are currently in is your reality, your destiny is totally different. Look at Dr. Ben Carson, based on the accounts he has given of his life, when he was in 5th grade he had straight F's and could not read or write. He also had a violent temper. Today, he is the top Neurosurgeon in the world and maybe the greatest surgeon to ever life. Dr. Carson is from the rough streets of Detroit, single Mother, you know, all the excuses that a lot of us use as to why we can't be successful. President Barack Obama, grew up poor and with a single Mother between Kansas and Hawaii as he grew into adulthood… He overcame his reality to Write His Own Destiny.

Let me finish this point with Allen Iverson, he had an extremely rough upbringing. Iverson's childhood home had raw sewage all over the floor from busted pipes. He went to jail for a fight at a bar in which he was completely innocent and lost all of his college scholarship offers except for the one he took, Georgetown. We all know what he did with that 1 offer. Iverson had a quote that perfectly sums up this message that I am giving you in this chapter. Iverson said when people would say to him, "*Man you got a 1 in a million chance at the NBA*", he would always respond "*Well, I am going to be that 1*".

Let me tell you the same thing. *Be that 1!* See it! Feel it! Believe It! Your NOW, only affects your tomorrow if you allow it! Truth be told, you should be thankful that you come from the gutter! As Lupe Fiasco put it *The Struggle / A sign that God loves you / Being Poor Teaches You How To Hustle*.

When you overcome the obstacles you will face in life and eventually write your own destiny, you are going to appreciate your journey. Where you are from will no longer be looked at as a burden, it will be looked at as a badge of honor. You are destined to make it, so don't worry about where you are from.

BIG PICTURE
Flipping The Scripts On Where You Are From

Jay Z gives you a message of strength in the verse:

"Alright but, I'm Different / Can't base what I am going to be off of what everybody isn't"

Again, you can't look at everyone around you and think that your fate is tied to theirs! What you see for yourself when you close your eyes and dream, you must go out and pursue it. Even if it means that you will be the 1st to do it, don't stop until the destiny that you always wanted is your reality!

Jay Z closes the verse saying:

"Just Whispering behind my back / No Vision / Lack of Ambition / So Whack"

Yes, you will have haters. People will tell you that can't, that you shouldn't. Why? They can't see it! *"No Vision..."* I honestly don't like calling people haters, I just think of them as people who can't see themselves doing what you are doing and because of this, they don't believe you will be able to do it.

Maybe it's the optimist in me - either way, make believers out of those who doubt your and their own abilities. You never know, when you reach your goal, they may believe that they can reach theirs…

It is not where you are from, it is where you are going!

Chapter 9
Discussion Questions

1.) <u>D.O.K. 2 Explain</u> How does the outlook of your friends on their future impact the way you visualize your personal future?

2.) <u>D.O.K. 3 Evaluate</u> Do you think or feel like your grades determine your future? Why? Explain the difference between determine and impact.

3.) <u>D.O.K. 3 Analyze</u> How do you feel about your neighborhood or community? Do you think it has an effect on your ability to "make it"?

4.) <u>D.O.K. 2 Explain</u> Have you ever been told that your chance to be something is 1 in a million? Did it deter you from pursuing your dream or goal?

5.) <u>D.O.K. 3 Evaluate</u> What do you feel is your biggest obstacle in your environment that you must overcome in order to be successful?

Common Core Standards

CCSS R.I. 8.3 Analyze how a text makes connections among and distinctions between individuals, ideas, or events (e.g., through comparisons, analogies, or categories).

CCSS R.I. 9 - 10.3 Analyze how the author unfolds an analysis or series of ideas or events, including the order in which the points are made, how they are introduced and developed, and the connections that are drawn between them.

CCSS R.I. 11 - 12.3 Analyze a complex set of ideas or sequence of events and explain how specific individuals, ideas, or events interact and develop over the course of the text.

Notes:

Rejecting The Narrative

Section 4:

Questioning How The Roles We Play and Things We Have Been Taught To Accept, Truly Align with Our Life Goals

A Message From J. Cole...

...There's all sorts of trauma from drama that children see
Type of *stuff* that normally would call for therapy
But you know just how it go in our community
Keep that *stuff* inside it don't matter how hard it be
Fast forward, them kids is grown and they blowing trees
And popping pills due to chronic anxiety
I been saw the problem but stay silent 'cause I ain't Jesus
This ain't no trial if you desire go higher please
But f*ck that now I'm older I love you 'cause you my friend
Without the drugs I want you be comfortable in your skin
I know you so I know you still keep a lot of *stuff* in
You running from yourself and you buying product again
I know you say it helps and no I'm not trying to offend
But I know depression and drug addiction don't blend
Reality distorts and then you get lost in the wind
And I done seen the combo take *brothers* off the deep end
One thing about your demons they bound to catch up one day
I'd rather see you stand up and face them than run away
I understand this message is not the coolest to say
But if you down to try it I know of a better way...
Meditate

Chapter 10
Smoking or Drinking Will Solve your Problems

I Smoke A Blunt To Take The Pain Out / Cause if I wasn't High I'd Probably Try To Blow My Brains Out / I'm Hopeless

Lord Knows by Tupac

This line from Pac speaks to a mind frame that is held by millions of people all across the world, not just people in our hoods. Ain't no escaping it, people will forever turn to the bottle or a blunt to get their mind off what they are going through. I have personally never tried it, that's 💯. TBH, I feel like it works. ONLY TEMPORARILY. It may take your mind off your problem but it does not solve your problem. Look, I already know that I am not going to shutdown the liquor industry nor am I going to get people to stop smoking with what I am about to write. However, I do think I can get you to rethink the reasons why and when you decide to do whatever you already made up your mind to do.

So what am I talking about? I am talking about the problems that we are trying to escape when we are getting drunk or high. I'll never be the one to tell you that what you are going through isn't hard. Life can be hard. I know that it is millions of people from all races going through it. Whether it is abusive parents, not enough food in the house, roaches in your crib, or the fact that drugs and gangs run your neighborhood. Whatever the case maybe, I know you are trying to find an escape from what is stressing you out. I also know that, weed and liquor are the easiest and most accessible ways to find that escape. That's real. I want to tell you a little story that I heard that may help you look at things a little different, alright? Here we go, it's called the Devil's Yard Sale.

<u>The Devil's Yard Sale</u>
One day the Devil is having a yard sale and on one particular table he has some tools. On this table he has the tools; lust, envy, fear, deceit (lying), hate and this really beat up tool with no price tag on it. So this guy is looking on the table and he is picking different tools up and looking at them and he comes to the tool that is beat up and since it has no label and price tag he is confused.

After a minute of trying to figure out what it is, he walks over to the Devil who is talking to someone at the sale and says, "Excuse me, I noticed this tool on your table and it appears that you have put it to great use, however it doesn't have a label or price tag on it, I would like to buy it, can you please tell me what it is?"

The Devil is in total shock and looks at the man and says, "Sir, I am sorry there must be a mistake, it has no label on it because it is not for sale, I am not sure how this even got out here, again my apologies for the confusion." The Devil begins to walk back towards the house to put the tool away, when the man stops and says, "What is that tool?" I see that it is worn out and you must use this a lot, I would like to know what it is?" The Devil goes over to the man and puts his arm around his shoulder as if to quiet him down. They walk into a corner of the garage and the Devil says to the man, "Okay, I will tell you what this tool is, however you can not buy it! This tool is my GREATEST TOOL, this tool is DISCOURAGEMENT.

Discouragement is my greatest tool because, no one know that this tool belongs to me and once I have used this on someone, they are vulnerable and all my other tools work without any resistance or push back from the person that I am using it on. Sir, once a person is discouraged or feeling hopeless, I can have my way with them! Anything that I want to do with them I have total access to when they are discouraged. Sir, discouragement is the ultimate highway to destruction."

I think this story perfectly applies to everyone. Think back to the last lines of the Tupac verse that I started with - I'm Hopeless. If that is not being discouraged then I don't know what is. We all have been discouraged at some point and felt low or really bad about ourselves. We all have sat in our room by ourselves and had what my Mother would call a "Pity Party". For some it is even worse, your entire life may feel like on big, unescapable nightmare. Please allow me to ask this question, how does getting high or drunk make it better?

I understand that you are discouraged but getting high or drunk will only alter your mental state for the moment, but once you come back down, what are you trying to escape is still going to be right where you left it. Don't trip, I don't want you to think that I am saying that your situation is hopeless, I am saying that trying to find a temporary fix is not a way to deal with what is going on. Let's be real about the situation, starting habits like smoking or drinking will only develop into other problems that will likely only create more discouragement in your life. I'm not bashing it because I don't do it, I am saying that you should look for a solution and not an escape. Smoking weed and drinking alcohol is an escape.

Say for instance you had a dog and he pooped in the middle of your room, would you clean it up or would you just put newspaper over it and walk around it? Eventually, covering it up ain't going to work, you are going to have to clean it up. Depending on how long you leave it there, you know it is going to leave a stain. Smoking and drinking is covering it up and not cleaning up your problems. The longer you try to ignore the problem in your life, the bigger the stain it will leave and the more discouraged you will become and you will feel just like Pac - "I'm Hopeless".

The Big Picture
Flip The Scripts On Drugs & Alcohol

I don't want you to think that I have went through this world without being stressed or that I haven't been put in a situation where I could have smoked or gotten drunk. I just chose not to do those things. I have pretty much bared my soul in this book, my Moms was 19 years old with 3 kids and we grew up on welfare. I have seen drive by shootings, people that I knew growing up have been murdered, I have had my share of problems. I just want you to do what I have done and that is stayed focused on the solution and not the problem. In most cases, the problem isn't one you created, however because you FEEL powerless, (not that you are powerless) you think that you can't do anything about it. That is not true, there is always a way to solve your problem. However, when we become DISCOURAGED, we are subject to more of the Devil's tricks and feel that we have no hope. Next time you feel DISCOURAGED, know that it is the Devil at work and only your Faith and your Focus will pull you through, not the bottle or the blunt… 💯!

Here are a few things that I would suggest that you do besides turning to drinking and smoking the next time you feel Discouraged:

1. Pray - Regardless of what you have been told or may feel about religion, you are God's child and you were created for a purpose. Pray - have faith and follow what you know is right. God will answer you prayers when it is time for them to be answered.

2. Write down how you feel. It doesn't have to be to anyone or for anyone else to see. Just right how you are feeling. A lot of times we feel stressed or angry because that fire we got in our chest that we can't get out and no one wants to listen to has us so frustrated. We have to let it out somehow, this is the feeling we try to smoke or drink away. Write about it, you will feel better even if you throw it away afterwards. Let it out, you will feel better.

3. Spend more time with your passion. If you like taking pictures, playing basketball, learning about dinosaurs, playing video games. Whatever it is, spend your time with what it is that gives you that peace. Something in your life makes you feel better when you do it, spend more time doing that.

4. Plan your future. Whatever it is that makes you discouraged must be addressed. My issue was my biological father, so I planned to have everything he didn't. I vowed to get my college degree and to be in my children's life. I worked daily at making sure that I would not lead a life that resembled his and I achieved that goal. Use your Discouragement as motivation to overcome whatever it is that has you feeling as Pac put it… Hopeless.

Chapter 10
Discussion Questions

1.) <u>D.O.K. 2 Analyze</u> Do you or anyone you know turn to drugs or alcohol to cope with problems? What are some other alternatives that could help a person deal with their problems?

2.) <u>D.O.K. 4 Create</u> Write 3 -5 sentences on a separate sheet of paper explaining your reaction to the Devil's Yard Sale?

3.) <u>D.O.K. 3 Evaluate</u> Tupac says "If I wasn't high I'd probably try to blow my brains out!" Does life ever make you feel like suicide or self medication are your only choices? Why or why not?

4.) <u>D.O.K. 3 Analyze</u> How do you deal with stress? What are some of the ways you can productively find solutions to your issues?

5.) <u>D.O.K. 4 Create</u> Write about a time that you gave someone who was discouraged advice? Can you use the same advice when you are discouraged?

Common Core Standards

CCSS R.I. 8.3 Analyze how a text makes connections among and distinctions between individuals, ideas, or events (e.g., through comparisons, analogies, or categories).

CCSS R.I. 9 - 10.3 Analyze how the author unfolds an analysis or series of ideas or events, including the order in which the points are made, how they are introduced and developed, and the connections that are drawn between them.

CCSS R.I. 11 - 12.3 Analyze a complex set of ideas or sequence of events and explain how specific individuals, ideas, or events interact and develop over the course of the text.

Notes:

We Often Try To Measure What Manhood is and What It Means To Be Tough or Hard. However, Manhood is Not Something That Can Be Measured. Instead We Must Begin To Accept All of Our Brothers as Just That, Brothers... When We Respect Everyone As If They Were Our Family We Will Begin To See The Healing Take Place, Which We So Desperately Need Within Our Community.

- Alan Gaines

Chapter 11
It Was How I Was Raised…

Meet Pat…

Pat is not your typical male. Pat is very shy and quiet but likes to be around people. Pat is about to turn 18 in a few months and is awaiting his acceptance letter from Morehouse, which is his 1st choice of Colleges. Pat is a good student so; while he is super anxious to hear his results, he is confident he will get in. Pat wishes he could speed up time and hurry up and get there because he feels that a person like him will be accepted and understood more in Atlanta.

From the time he started school in Kindergarten he has been ridiculed and talked about for being different. Pat knows that he is not like most boys. However, he also never understood why people are so mean and said cruel things about him as he grew up. Pat was and has always been very nice to people. Pat has always been the type who is willing to share his things and help others in need. Definitely not one to be confused with an alpha male, Pat has always tried to stay in the background and go unnoticed. Well, that did not always work. Somehow or someway people always found ways to have a problem with the way that he "is". All of Pat's friends were girls because the boys didn't think it was cool to have a friend like "that." So the bullying went on for years and although Pat never got immune to it, as he entered his senior year of high school, Pat finally felt he was in the home stretch and the bullying would soon end. Being that Pat was a good student and he had finished most of his required classes, so he didn't have to go to school the entire day during his senior year.

Well, there was one person who felt the need to keep bothering Pat, his name was Donald. Donald was one of the more popular kids in the school and he was always ready to fight or start some trouble. Donald was more than just your typical bully, he came from a family that sold drugs and ran with gangs. Being that Donald was trap affiliated, he always had money and could afford to stay in some fresh J's and gold chains to deck out his uniforms that he had to wear for school. Donald went by D and he was about 5'11 and 260 pounds, dark skinned and usually kept a scowl on his face.

Now, the beef between D and Pat really has no merit but there was one incident that D has held on to and could be the reason that Donald still finds the need to bully Pat. It was Freshman year and they were in Ms. Griffins' English Class and the class was having a vocabulary word competition and Pat was facing Donald. Pat was usually so shy that he would miss the word on purpose so he could just sit down and be out of the game. Well on this particular day, Donald took all of his Freshman testosterone up to the board with him and felt that he would embarrass Pat. Pat was a bit naïve and had no idea that Donald was going to try to make fun of him because right before class in the hallway, Donald's things had fallen out of his book bag and Pat helped him pick them up. Donald, was very nice and told Pat "Good looking bro, that was cool of you to help." Pat responded, "Oh, your welcome." Pat then got the door and Donald walked in and Pat followed behind him and went to his seat in the front. So as Donald walked to the back, his boys start clowning him a little bit for walking in the classroom with Pat. Pat missed all this as he is getting his materials out for class. However, Donald didn't and he doesn't like being clowned at all, so he is highly upset about the jokes. Donald is going to make someone pay.

So when Ms. Griffin called Donald and Pat up to the board for the game, the class makes the "Oooooohhhhhhhhh" noise and Donald gets up and switches with his right hand open and up by his shoulders all the way from the back of the room in an obvious mockery of Pat. Pat sees Donald walking and makes up his mind that instead of missing the question like he normally does, Pat says to himself, "Not Today" so when Ms. Griffin ask them to spell the word llama and give the definition, Pat was careful to place two L's on his whiteboard along with the correct definition. Donald, who is a smart kid and just never applies himself, was careless and only put one L in llama. Ms. Griffin looked at both boards and awarded two points to Pat's team and only one point to Donald's. Pat's team let out a "YES" and Pat, being caught up in the moment, strutted back to his desk with a tough guy limp in mockery of Donald. Everyone laughed at the gesture and Donald.

Now Donald's ego is bruised and he goes over to approach Pat, quickly intervening, Ms. Griffin calls "Donald" who stops in his tracks. "Uh, go sit down Mr. Perkins, when you mocked him he didn't try to fight you… Maybe you should study your words and you wouldn't be so upset."

Donald knows Ms. Griffin is right and seeing that she is a highly respected teacher, Donald goes and has a seat. However, he still hasn't let that moment from 4 years ago in their Freshman year go, so to this day, Donald still has it out for Pat. They say life has an odd way of working itself out, well let me take you inside the day that changed both Pat and Donald's lives forever...

It was homecoming day of their senior year and Pat wasn't really into all the school spirit stuff, however his best friend Tyronda was running for Homecoming Queen and she was pretty much a shoe in being that she was the most popular girl in the school. Tyronda had been Pat's friend since the second grade and was one of the few people that would stick up for Pat over the years. Pat hung around after his morning classes to be there for Tyronda and for the most part was trying to be his usual low key self when all the other seniors were hanging around at lunch taking pictures and signing each others yearbooks. Donald was about two lunch tables over kicking it with his bros and his girlfriend Chante who happened to be Tyronda's cousin. So Pat is becoming rather bored and since he has always been image conscious and not really one for pictures he decided that he was ready to go and was going to make up an excuse to tell Tyronda that he would just see her later tonight at the football game. As he is walking over towards Tyronda, Donald, who is always outspoken and usually cruel to people he feels are lames, sees Pat walking over and out of nowhere begins singing very loudly, The For The "D" Challenge Song. In typical bully fashion, instead of saying what he would do, Donald is putting Pat in the lyrics, which has everyone laughing. Both Tyronda and Chante tell Donald to knock it off to which Donald replies, "Ok, ok, I was just having a little fun with the fruit cake..." Chante punches him in the chest getting him to stop and then Donald goes into the Beyonce – "I ain't sorry, I ain't sorry" which only arouses more laughter from everyone around. Pat is annoyed, but pretty much used to it so he just bites his tongue tells Tyronda that he will see her tonight and hurries off.

Let's fast forward a few hours to halftime and the homecoming festivities. As expected Tyronda won Homecoming Queen and Pat is there down by the entrance to the field and is waiting for Tyronda to congratulate her and take a few pictures. And although Pat loves hanging out with his friends at the games, he doesn't stick around for the second half of the game. Football is not a sport that he is into so he quickly find his escape and heads home on his bike.

The bike ride took all of 18 minutes to get home and when he comes through the door, he yells out to his mom that he made it home safe. Oddly, he hears a few other voices in the kitchen talking with his mom. Pat goes into the kitchen to see who his mom is talking to.

As he walks into the kitchen he sees his Uncle Rod sitting at the table across from his mother and immediately he is happy to see his Uncle who gets up to embrace him with a loud "Nephew". Pat responds, "Wsup Uncle Rod!" and the two embrace. Pat scans over to the refrigerator behind his Uncle and notices someone in the freezer part getting ice for his beer but with the door in his face he can't make out who it is. So as the person closes the door on the freezer and turns around, Pat sees that it is Vic, his Uncle's close friend and former roommate. At the sight of Vic, Pat goes into immediate frozen fear and pees on himself! Vic attempts to speak to the frozen and terrified Pat saying "Wsup Pat?" as he takes a sip from his glass full of beer. Pat immediately runs to his room.

Pat's mom is completely confused and abruptly goes after Pat. No luck, Pat has locked himself in his bedroom and is refusing to open the door. Pat tells his Mom that he is not coming out of his room and he just wants to sleep and they would talk about everything in the morning. That isn't good enough for her, she demands that he open the door and let her in. Pat again refuses and begins to push things over in his room having a full blown emotional meltdown. Pat's mom knows that her son is bullied at school and she has become accustomed to him having frustrated outbursts. Usually, after he calms down they talk out what has happened. This is different and his Mother knows it. She is in total shock seeing that he is almost 18 and he just wet himself. She gets a feeling that it is probably best to give him space and let him calm down. So she goes back to the kitchen and tell Rod and Vic they have to go.

Rod gives his sister a big hug and kiss and says to her "Yo I know P (what he calls Pat) is different but you sure he going to be alright?" She replies, "I don't know... this feels a little different Rod, I'll keep you posted when I get to the bottom of this..." Rod tells her "Ok, well you know if you or P need anything, Sis I got you, real talk..." Mom replies, "Yeah I know, but let me see what's wrong with my baby alright…"

Rod, trying to give reassurance, tells her, "You know me and Vic love P, he was like our 3rd roommate back in the day when we used to watch him. You was working nights as a CNA going for your LPN. Pat used to be how Vic and me would get all the girls back in the day… Remember Vic?" Rod turns and looks at a visibly nervous Vic who is waiting by the door who only can muster, "Mmmhhmm" Vic is now trying to hurry Rod out… "Bro let's rock, she got things to take care of." Mom says to Rod "Look, I'll call you in the morning. Just let me handle this…" Rod and Vic walk out. Mom locks the door and makes her way back towards Pats' room.

Mom knocks at the door and says "Pat, they gone. Can we talk now?" "Ma, I just want to clean myself up and go to sleep." Pat responds. Mom is careful not to push, "Ok, well I am off tomorrow so I will get up and make you some breakfast and we can talk it out, Ok?" "Alright Ma" Pat says through the tears as he sits on the floor with his back against his bed. His Mom slowly walks away from the door and into her room. She goes to close the door only to open it back and yell to Pat, "There is some dinner in the oven and by the way you got some mail from Morehouse on the table in the kitchen. I was going to open it but I know how you are about me going in your stuff… Anyway, I love you baby, it's going to be okay, whatever it is… alright…" Pat is emotionally drained right now and yells "I know Ma, love you too!" In hopes that she will just go to bed and that he can too, he knows that tomorrow is going to be very heavy and emotional because he has to reveal what is behind what just happened.

Pat pulls himself up from the floor after about 10 minutes of just trying to collect his thoughts. Finally, Pat goes to the bathroom and showers. His mind is racing about all the stuff that has happened today. He can't wait to sit down and read his acceptance letter from Morehouse, that good news is going to go perfect with his dinner, Pat says to himself. His mom cooked stuffed chicken, which is his favorite. Pat thinks to himself, "At least two good things can come out of this otherwise terrible day."

Well by now, Pat has cleaned up and has gotten his food from the oven. He closes the oven door and looks at the stove and notices it is barely 9:45pm. Pat cuts off the stove that was on low just to keep his food warm. He sits down and takes the aluminum foil off of his plate and begins eating. Pat fumbles through the mail and finds the letter addressed to him from Morehouse. Pat opens it up and begins to read…

Dear Pat,

Thank you for your interest in Morehouse College. Unfortunately, at this time we regret to inform you...

Pat drops the letter and his head simultaneously. Pat begins to question God… "Why me, Lord" "What have I done to deserve all this pain" Pat is suddenly becoming overwhelmed with the thought that he will be stuck in his hometown forever. He had his heart set on going to Atlanta and starting over, now that is all out the window. The tears begin to flow down his cheek and as they reach his chin, Pat becomes enraged! He slams his fork into the perfectly baked piece of chicken and angrily gets up from the table, knocking over the chair and heads towards his room. He goes into his backpack for a pen and his notebook. He sits and writes something on the paper and after writing the short note he finds some clothes to put on. Pat puts on a black hoodie and some jeans. He sits back on the bed to put on his all black huaraches and after putting on both shoes, he tears the paper he wrote out of his notebook, folds it and puts it in his pocket. Pat hurries to the closet by the front door and goes into the inside pocket of an old coat that keeps his mothers 9mm handgun. His mother has kept the gun there and told him about it because her job has her doing swing shifts. His Mom doesn't like the idea of him being alone without protection if she is working midnights. This is a decision that his Mom may soon regret.

By now, Pat is out of the house and on his bike, tears are still streaming down his cheek as he has become overwhelmed by what he feels is the dim light of his future. Pat has been riding for 20 minutes and comes to the river that runs through his town. Pat rides his bike off the road and down the small hill to the shore of the water. He drops his bike and begins pacing back and forth, contemplating does he want to do it. He thinks to himself "God must not love me, my daddy has never been in my life, you let Vic do that to me, I didn't get into Morehouse! I hate myself!" Pat reaches into his pocket and grabs the letter, and then he goes into his hoodie and brings out the gun. Pat puts the barrel of the gun in his mouth. The tears are now just flowing, he put his finger on the trigger and right as he begins to squeeze… He hears a car slam on the breaks…

Pat turns to look in the direction of the loud noise. The car loses control and is going head first into the lake. Pat drops both the gun and the letter and runs toward the sinking car. Pat dives into the lake and sees that the driver of the car has passed out. Luckily, the windshield shattered on impact of the water and Pat is able to swim inside and get the driver out. Pat gets the unconscious body to shore a few feet from where he was about to commit suicide. Pat begins to give the young man mouth to mouth trying to bring him back to life. Pat is giving chest compressions and after a 3rd blow into his mouth, the young man begins to cough and gasp for air. Pat musters up enough strength to turn the bigger guy onto his side and as the water begins to spew from the drivers mouth, who is slowly regaining consciousness, Pat reaches into his pocket to retrieve his phone so he can call 911 – luckily its a Galaxy so it is waterproof.

As Pat is talking to the operator, giving them details of the crash and where to send the ambulance, the driver recognizes Pat's voice and turns toward him and tries to say "Pat" but water is still in his system so only a "Puh" comes out before he coughs up more water. The coughing sound turns a concerned Pat in the direction of the driver who has by now made it to his knees, yet still spitting trying to clear the water from inside his mouth and lungs. Pat still trying to help kneels down to one knee and tries to help him up to his feet. As this is happening, the total shock of witnessing a car crash and having to save someone's life is beginning to wear off and Pat looks at who he has been helping this whole time and with a totally stunned voice says "D"???! (What everyone calls Donald) Donald knew he recognized that voice and finds the strength to say "Yeah Pat, its me…"

Donald continues talking as he tries to collect himself, "Thanks for all this bro, real talk you saved my life!" Donald coughs and spits out more water. Pat is taken back and worried that Donald may try to hurt him because he gave him mouth to mouth so Pat says "Man I am glad you are alright, you know I had to give you…" Donald cuts him off, "Yeah I know and that's what I am saying thank you for… I ain't worried about that ish, I'm just glad I'm alive." Donald by now is up to one knee and as he is gathering himself get up on his feet he notices the crumpled up paper and the gun. Donald knows it's not his gun so he grabs it and the paper also. Donald is trying to wrap his mind around why Pat of all people would have a gun. So Donald is searching for answers when he ask "Is this yours Pat?" referring to the gun. Not really waiting for Pat's response he opens the piece of paper and begins to read…

> "Ma, I love you... I'm so sorry and I know this hurts but now you can live your life and not have to worry about me and the shame I bring you because I am gay... I love you Ma... P.S. It was Vic"

A confused Donald looks up at Pat and says "Bro, you were out here about to... kill yourself?" An emotionally drained Pat has started crying again and through the world wind of all the emotions, didn't even have the strength to stop Donald from reading the letter, so when he heard Donald's question, he simply nods at him as he wipes away tears.

Donald asks a visibly shaken Pat, "Bro you were going to kill yourself? For what?" Pat can see the concern in Donald's face and being that he is emotionally vulnerable at the moment, Pat decides to open up to Donald, of all people. Pat says:

> "When I was 4 years old my mom went back to school to get her LPN and my Uncle Rod and his roommate Vic would watch me. My Mom thought I needed a man in my life, especially since my Dad cut out on my Mom before I was born. My Uncle had a job so a lot of the time I would be alone with Vic. Vic began touching me and making me do things with him for as long as I could remember. Vic molested me almost every day for 7 years. Vic told me that I he would kill my Uncle Rodney in his sleep and he would kill my Mom as she came to pick me up if I ever told anyone. My Mom and my Uncle Rod are the only family I got and without them what would I do? The first 4 years, he just touched me and made do things to him. When I was about 9 he started forcing me to have sex with him... I HATED IT! But I was too scared to ever say anything. Vic would call me names and play games with my head about what he wanted to do to me. He always would threaten me about what he would do to me if anyone ever found out about what he was doing to me… It was horrible! I lived terrified, I wet the bed until I was about 14.

And y'all didn't make it any better at school, talking about me everyday calling me a faggot every day. Honestly, with what I was going through at home, what y'all did at school was nothing. When I was 11 Vic moved away and everything stopped. By that time I was already considered the "Gay Boy" at school and there was nothing I could do about it. To be honest, I was just happy that Vic wasn't there to mess with me. I am gay, if that is what you want to call it because I like boys, but I don't know if I naturally like boys or if I like boys because of what Vic did to me. I have lived my whole life in fear and I have been tortured and bullied since my 1st day of Kindergarten. I always wanted a male friend to hang with but since everyone thought I was gay, I have never had any males my age to hang with. Since I was the "Gay Boy" no one ever gave me a chance to do anything, all those conversations y'all had about basketball in class — I knew every stat from LeBron, KD, Kobe, D Wade, D Rose, Steph... everybody. My Uncle Rod had me watching the games and even took me out and taught me how to play. Believe it or not, I can play Donald, but once I got that label as "Gay" no one would ever pick me up for anything sports related unless it was PE and they had to. I was so afraid of everything, I just acted like I am not good at anything so people won't pick on me more. I know that sounds crazy but, imagine living your life in fear at home and being bullied at school. Donald, I don't know what life is, honestly, because I have never been happy. That has been taken from me. I go out places with my mother and people look at my Mom in disgust because I am gay. As if she did something wrong. She tells me to ignore it but I know that the looks we get bother her, embarrassing my Mom really hurts the worst. Everyday, I wake up feeling like I am a walking disappointment to everyone. I feel so worthless all the time. My childhood was spent as a sex object for a family friend and the punching bag for every kid in school who needed to bully someone to make themselves feel better. You don't know how many nights I have cried trying to ask God, Why?

Why did he choose me to endure this cruelty? My mom said never to question God, but after I found out a couple of hours ago that I didn't get into Morehouse. I honestly don't see the point of living anymore. I was so looking forward to moving away and getting a fresh start, but now that ain't going to happen so I gotta stay here... I'd rather die than stay here... That's real talk, I hate it here and since God didn't answer that prayer, I had the gun in my mouth about to kill myself right before you crashed because I am sure that God hates me..."

Donald, who has shed a few tears hearing all that Pat has been through, stops Pat, "Hold on, Bro, God doesn't hate you, God don't hate nobody. I mean I can't answer why you been through so much messed up stuff, but I know God don't hate anybody bro. I mean, look at what just happened, you saved my life right after I had an accident that because God saw fit to intervene, saved yours. God loves everybody Bro, even me and I do wild stuff all the time. I be robbing folks and selling drugs. But God loved me enough to not let me die in that lake a minute ago and he had you of all people save me. That ain't no coincidence. Before I go on, man I am so sorry for all the messed up stuff I did to you over the years, Bro. Had I known all that, I wouldn't have let nobody mess with you, nor would I have been treating you like shit all these years…"

An annoyed Pat cuts Donald off, "That's the part that kills me, D! Why can't anyone just see me, as a person, Gay or Straight, aren't I a human? Isn't that enough? Part of the reason, I never let anyone know what has happened is because, I am going to be looked at like a charity case. I just want to feel like a regular human, being, not the "Gay Boy" not the boy who was molested for years… I just want people to see Pat… When! When! Huh? When will being who I am just be enough and worthy of being treated with some decency?!" Pat walks back toward his bike frustrated and tired still lost because he has no idea as to what is next.

Donald is stunned because he never looked at it from that perspective. Donald tells Pat, *"Yo, wait up, look, I never thought about it like that until you just said that, honestly. My whole family is against gay people…*

Ever since I was little, I was told not to be no punk! Don't cry when something hurts or I get emotional. 'Stop being soft,' man you know what I am talking about. I was raised to be hard, because weak niggas get took and treated like a punk... Bro, it was just the way I was raised."

Pat again intervenes, this time yelling, *"Well maybe the way you were raised is the problem!"*

In that moment Donald watches Pat walk up the hill and get back onto his bike. Donald has no response because he now realizes that how he thought, although it is widely accepted, has been the thing that has caused Pat and people like Pat to live and feel depressed and worthless...

The Big Picture
Flipping The Scripts On Homophobia

In the Black community, especially among young men, very few things are viewed in a worse light than being homosexual. I will admit I was a part of the culture that made fun of and picked on kids for being homosexual growing up. I vividly remember what made me stop talking about homosexuals, it was the movie Blind Faith. I watched it during the summer going into my 9th grade year and in this beautifully written film, you go the vast majority of the film thinking that this kid is the victim of a race crime to later find out that his homosexuality was the true reason this young man is going through this ordeal.

Now, this film humanized the situation for me in regards to developing empathy for people who are either by birth or by choice homosexual. I will leave that up for debate and regardless of how you view the topic. However, the fact still remains at the end of the day that people who are homosexuals are just that... People! Regardless of your position on the matter, the fact that God has created them means that you should treat them as such at all cost. PERIOD!

I wrote this chapter for many reasons, mainly to shed light on how it may feel to be a homosexual male growing up in an all black community that definitely frowns upon and shuns people who are gay. I also wanted to open the door to address sexual abuse in males, a topic that is largely taboo and lots of people avoid discussing. We can't keep ignoring it because it is happening at a very high rate. I encourage anyone who has been molested or who is being molested to speak up and let someone know. Also, by keeping quiet you are empowering your abuser to feel safe to abuse someone else.

I honestly don't know what or how this story will impact people, but I do know that the issues that I have discussed from Bullying and Homosexuality to Molestation all need to be addressed. I pray that this helps many people view others from something other than societies lens of Gay or Straight, Weak or Hard, but simply as a…. HUMAN…

Chapter 11
Discussion Questions

1.) <u>D.O.K. 2 Explain</u> How do your feelings for Pat change throughout the story?

2.) <u>D.O.K. 2 Analyze</u> Do you know anyone like D in the story? Is his behavior acceptable? Why or Why not?

3.) <u>D.O.K. 3 Evaluate</u> Why does Pat not getting into Morehouse make him want to commit suicide?

4.) <u>D.O.K. 4 Evaluate</u> What is the problem Pat has with how D was raised? Is homophobia taught in your home or neighborhood?

5.) <u>D.O.K. 4 Create</u> You Write The Ending! The author doesn't tell us how things end up for Pat or Vic, what do you think should happen? Write 2 - 3 Paragraphs Ending the Story!

Common Core Standards

CCSS RL 8.3 Analyze how particular lines of dialogue or incidents in a story or drama propel the action, reveal aspects of a character, or provoke a decision.

CCSS RL 9 - 10.3 Analyze how complex characters (e.g., those with multiple or conflicting motivations) develop over the course of a text, interact with other characters, and advance the plot or develop the theme.

CCSS RL 11 - 12.3 Analyze the impact of the author's choices regarding how to develop and relate elements of a story or drama (e.g., where a story is set, how the action is ordered, how the characters are introduced and developed).

Notes:

Flip The Scripts & Write Your Own Destiny

Section 5:

A Strategy For Self Empowerment

Even When You Pray,

The Next Day You
Gotta Try,

Can't Wait For Nobody To Come Down Out
The Sky...

You Gotta Realize That The Worlds A Test...

You Can Only Do Your Best and Let Him Do
The Rest...

You Got Yo Life, You Got Yo Health, So Quit
Procrastinating and Push It Yourself...

- Cee Lo Green
In Due Time

Chapter 12
Write Your Own Destiny

This is your life. THIS IS YOUR LIFE. THIS. IS. YOUR. LIFE. There is no such thing as a 2nd life. People get 2nd chances but there is no such thing as a 2nd LIFE. So as they, HANDLE WITH CARE. Let me give you a few suggestions that will allow you to Flip The Scripts…

1. Know Thyself

Life was frustrating to me until I found out what it meant to be Black in America. I wrote this book specifically to young Black males, but I fully understand that much of what I have written will go across racial lines. So if you are a Hispanic American, Latin American or any other minority trying to figure it out in this place called America, my advice is that you learn your history to understand yourself.

If you are Black, it is super important that you learn about Pre Colonial Africa and how we come from a continent full of vast resources and Kings and Queens. In Africa our ancestors built dynasties and cultures that people still try to mimic (copy) until this very day. In Africa, we had scientist and engineers who built structures and systems that made life convenient for all people. These facts along with many others have been buried under what America tells us is our beginning, as people held as slaves in this country. We must understand the psychological effects of making a group of people believe that we started out as slaves has had on the way we view ourselves.

More importantly, knowing the history of your people, will help you properly understand the oppression that they have faced both here in America and across the world. For Black males, when you learn about the works of Ida B. Wells, you will understand that her recordings of lynchings of Black people over 150 years ago were the original seeds of what you see today as the #BlackLivesMatter Movement. When you find out that Martin Luther King Jr. and Malcolm X led a Civil Rights movement that was only asking that America uphold a promise that was made to them on behalf of President Lincoln when he issued the Emancipation Proclamation 100 years earlier, you will understand the magnitude of the election of President Barack Obama. There are countless of benefits to knowing all that you can about yourself and in my opinion it is the place you must start 1st if you are going to Write Your Own Destiny.

2. Find Your Motivation

Shout out to Eric Thomas or ET The Hip Hop Preacher as he is known, for the inspiration on this one. He calls it "What is your Why?" The principle is basically who or what motivates you to do your very best. For me, it is my beautiful wife and 4 wonderful children. Originally, it was my mother. My Mom always wanted to be a teacher, now that I have fulfilled that dream and goal, I have moved on. I am now motivated to future success for the very best of my family.

Who or what motivates you? Who or what is the one thing that you are going to rely on to get through those tough times or dark hours when the weight of the world has you down? When you sitting in the Principal's office, the back of the police car or your Mom is talking about putting you out the house because you simply will not do right and she is tired and fed up with your actions, what is going to bring you through these tough times and get your focus back? Someone or something has to be motivating you that will keep you from giving up. There is a saying that goes. "To you the world may mean nothing, but to someone else, you may mean the world." Life may seem worthless while you are down, but I am sure you are very important to someone.

Who looks up to you? Who is watching your every move? They're maybe someone out there who is modeling their "game" after yours. I don't know the circumstance that you are in, however, you must have a motive or a purpose that will drive you toward success and excellence. You must find your motivation in either someone or something that you want out of life, that will prepare you when the Devil uses his tool of DISCOURAGEMENT the next time you find yourself in a bad spot. Knowing what motivates you will keep your eyes focused on the finish line and not the hurdle.

When I was in college, I remember thinking about my little brother EJ when I had a paper due Friday but Thursday was Ladies Night at Freelon's (A popular club in Jackson, MS) and everyone was in the cafe talking about how crunk (what we said back then, now y'all say lit) it was going to be. I wanted to go bad but I knew that school was more important and I wanted to be able to show my little brother that getting a degree could be done because I am going to do it.

That is motivation, I had no doubts about my ability - just needed a "Why" to keep me on track to make the right decisions. Motivation without direction can feel like pressure. Let's stay here for a second while I explain the difference between pressure and motivation.

Pressure is when you doubt your ability to complete a task that you know you can because you are worried about people you love looking down on you. Motivations is when you focus on the smiles and love you are going to get from those same people when you finish the task… Pressure is associated with FEAR. Motivation is associated with COURAGE. If I haven't given you this one already, let me give it to you now. The word FEAR can be broken into an Acronym - F.alse E.vidence A.ppearing R.eal - I have been using that one with my students ever since I came across it in a book a few years ago. What you see as Pressure could easily be seen as motivation if you adjust your lense.

Life is centered around the law of opposites and often times people mistake motivation and well wishes from loved ones for pressure simply because they doubt themselves. Whether it is the lady at the church, your Auntie, Grandma, your Old Coach, your favorite Uncle, whoever it is, you must realize that they see the potential in you to do great things. You must see it too. When you find your Motivation or as ET calls it your WHY, you will have the greatest tool against DISCOURAGEMENT. Your WHY is going to be that little angel on your shoulder telling you to make the right choice, if you listen to it, you will be fine, but 1st you must find it.

3. Find Your Passion, It Will Lead You To Your Purpose

What is the one thing that you could do everyday, never get paid for it and be completely happy doing it? I like to think that the answer to that question for everyone is their passion. Mine is helping people. I could help people for free all day everyday and never get paid for it and be completely happy doing it. However, in this society I would be homeless because I need income to provide the things needed in the home. So, I have to find a way to make money from my passion.

I don't know what skill God has blessed you with, it may even be more than just one. Write down the things that you are really good at and more than likely those are your gifts. After that, find the one that you feel the strongest about or enjoy the most. More than likely, that is your passion. You may love to draw, sing, dance, argue, take pictures, work with your hands, whatever it is that you feel passionate about is what you must do with your life. When I say feel, I mean that you are emotionally connected to it, you can't escape it, you get urges to do it, the feeling of doing it consumes you. You get urges to do it just like you have cravings for food, whatever that "IT" is, is your passion.

That "IT" is likely connected to your purpose, because your passion is always connected to your purpose. Not to get all spiritual but God put us here for a reason. You are reading these words for a reason. It is easy to work in your passion when you are walking in your purpose. My entire life, I saw things differently, most people used to think that I was trying to do it on purpose or just to be difficult. I wasn't, it was just how I looked at things, now that I am older, I have realized that my ability to look at things beyond what appears on the surface is going to help me change the lives of millions of people. Me writing this for you is allowing me to let my light shine. I want your light to do the same. Shine on!

Find that thing that you love to do and do it, no matter what other people think of it. If you love it, do it and don't think twice about it. A lot of brothers can really sing but because people think it is soft, the never let their voice be heard. God gave you these abilities for a reason, use them. I have heard people say that if your doing what you love then you can't call it work. Well, I say the same to your, find a way to do that which you love, then you will never work a day in your life.

I heard this while listening to Bob Proctor: "God's gift to you is more talent and ability than you will ever use in one lifetime. Your gift to God is to develop and utilize as much of that talent and ability as you can, in this lifetime." He is quoting Steve Bow, however, this is very fitting for the point I am making. Repay God for Your Gifts… Find Your Passion, Live Your Purpose.

4. Visualize Success

I can't think of nothing more critical to overcoming obstacles in life, especially those of poverty and life in the hood than, EXPOSURE. To me, it is an absolute must, that you find a way to travel beyond your neighborhood and see nice homes, clean streets and big buildings. I think it is important to see more than just the fancy and flashy things you see on TV. You need to see real people, not celebrities, living the lifestyle that you deserve to live. I'll repeat that - YOU DESERVE to live.

Seeing other people live the way that you should, hopefully will invoke, (develop) the desire within you to have and do more than you are currently doing. One of the major flaws of living in the hood or in poverty all together, is that pretty much everyone you know is living the same way. This creates a false sense of hopelessness that too many people fall victim to. To put it plainly, things in your neighborhood are so messed up, you feel like this is all you deserve and that it is what God intended for your life. That is not true, you were made for more.

I know it sounds like I am blowing smoke or selling you a dream when I say this, however, you must see it for yourself. Living a 1st class lifestyle must be visualized in your mind before your will live it in your reality. I'm not talking crazy, that is why I started this with EXPOSURE. Seeing life beyond your community will help you create that image in your mind and subconsciousness. You must visualize yourself being successful well before you have the success in the physical form. I am speaking of the Law of Attraction. Everything you see in the world started as an idea in someone's mind. Your success is exactly the same, you must visualize it.

This book, started in my head and I have a very clear image of you reading it as you hold it in your hands. Believe it or not, I see you reading this right now. I see the changes in your thinking that have begun to occur because of the different ideas that I have raised in this book. My purpose of writing this was to change lives, it's working… That is why you have to start to see yourself living and doing the things that will bring the success in your life that you desire.

Come on, we have all heard, you can do whatever you put your mind to. Whatever the mind can conceive, it can achieve. This is more than just some corny saying that your teacher would tell you in school to make you do better. This is a reality of life and the actual formula for success. Think about a building or a home for a second, how do they all start? Exactly, a blueprint or design, before the land is cleared or the dirt is turned over, someone has thought about how the finished product is going to look and put that idea on a piece of paper. That is also, exactly why you see that building turn out the way it does in the end, because every inch came from the vision.

You must do the same with your life. You have to begin creating the plan for success down to the smallest detail. Being that this is your life, you are the designer, engineer and construction worker of your own success. Thoughts become actions no matter how you want to look at it. So now that you are aware of this, I want you to think long and hard on ways that you can create the life that you want. See every detail of it, see it clearly, feel yourself doing it. Get so emotionally connected to it that it feels real. It should feel like that dream when you found a bunch of money only to wake up and it is gone. You are mad at the dream because it felt so real. That is how you must visualize your success, you have to feel it.

You are going to have to become obsessed with you goals. You hear people all the time say "I never thought about it like that". While they are saying that, they have a look on their face as if a whole new world has been opened up to them. Well, let me say it to you this way, most people don't reach their goals and dreams because they never think about them like that. Most people never really think about what they want in life, so when they are asked the question of "What do you want to be when you grow up?" You tend to get the same cliche answers; NBA, NFL, Doctor, Fireman, etc… Respectable answers that people are going to pretty much leave you alone when you give them that answer. However, the people giving these answers are not putting in hours working on their jump shot, running routes for football, studying medicine or learning about the life of a firefighter. People who are truly pursuing their passion, rarely get that question because you already know what they want to do because they are always doing it.

I'll never forget the day I asked my Dad (actually my Stepdad - but he has been with my mother since she was pregnant with me, so he is the only father I know) to be honest with me. I asked him did he think that I could make it to the NBA. He told me… NO. I was crushed, because I felt that he didn't believe in me. I told y'all I was good in basketball - so I asked him, "Why Not?" He told me that I "didn't have the intangibles." I had "too many other things that I was doing that were going to keep me from making it to the league." He told me the people who are going to the NBA are spending their time practicing outside of practice on their game and getting better. He said that I spent too much time playing video games, chasing girls and the fact that I played football the entire summer after AAU. I wasn't putting in the time that it took to get to the NBA. I appreciated his honesty then, but my mind was too small to see what he meant with what he was saying. I felt that he was saying that I didn't have what it took, when the truth was he was saying that I wasn't doing what it takes to get to the NBA. I wasn't envisioning my success and putting in the work to make it a reality. My picture was too crowded with other distractions. Put your minds eye on what you want, think about it relentlessly then work endlessly until it becomes your reality.

5. NEVER. EVER. GIVE. UP.

I want to say that I wish what I was telling you to do was easy, but in all honesty, I don't wish it were easy. What I do wish is, that more people had the courage to see it through. The main purpose of this book is to make you believe beyond any doubt that what you want out of life can be yours… If you are willing to sacrifice for it. There is a quote that I can up with that I often share with my players: "Success is the result of hardwork and dedication. Only those who are willing to commit to it and sacrifice for it, will ever enjoy it."

The road to success is not going to be easy bro and it shouldn't be. If it were easy, I know for a fact we would not appreciate it. It is like something someone gives you and something you buy with your own money. When someone gives you something, you don't care for it the same way as the things that you had to work for yourself. Success is the same way, which is why you can never give up on your dreams. Setbacks and obstacles are going to come and if you don't look at them with the right frame of mind, they will quickly turn into the Devil's greatest tool… Discouragement. We must strengthen ourselves to push through it.

I firmly believe that there is no such thing as failure, only quitting. I don't believe you ever fail at anything, you just stop trying and as a result your goal wasn't accomplished. Any way you want to look at it, you determined the result by your actions. Let me say that again, YOU DETERMINED THE RESULT BY YOUR ACTIONS.

Howard Schultz the owner of Starbucks Coffee was told no, over 200 times before he got someone to believe in his coffee bar idea. We see how well that turned out… He NEVER GAVE UP.

Thomas Edison tried over 1,000 times to create the light bulb, before he figured it out. They asked him how did it feel to fail over 1,000 times, he responded "I did not fail once, the light bulb was an invention with 1,000 steps." No need to go into how important the light bulb is… HE NEVER GAVE UP.

Jay Z, who grew up in the projects in Brooklyn, 1st album Reasonable Doubt, which people today regard as his best and a classic, flopped when it was 1st released. Good thing he saw himself successful despite what other people felt. Jay Z re-released it, it went multi platinum and now he owns nightclubs, part of the Brooklyn Nets, a sports marketing agency, Roc Nation music, the list goes on… HE NEVER GAVE UP.

Floyd Mayweather Jr., who grew up poor in Grand Rapids Michigan, who tells the story of his Dad selling drugs to his Mom, Dad was in prison, despite all this, Floyd kept his mind on becoming TBE. The Best Ever. Floyd walked through knee high snow every day after school and on weekends to the gym to work on his boxing skills. Floyd made over $300,000,000 for one 36 minute fight. He NEVER GAVE UP.

I can go on and on with people who overcame the odds and went from Rags to Riches as they say. I'm telling you that you can too. All these people I am telling you about, saw their success 1st. They started by knowing themselves, then they found their why, sought out their passion and purpose. They created a vision of success and worked relentlessly until it became their reality.

Yes, you are going to have haters and doubters. You are going to doubt yourself at times, you are going to feel like it is never going to happen. There will be times that you are going to get so close and then you are going to come up short. The unexpected is going to happen, you are going to lose a loved one somewhere along the journey. You may have a child during your road to success, Bro, life is going to happen. I would be lying to you if I said it was not. Either way, if you keep that vision of what you want crystal clear in your mind and never stop pursuing it, you will have what you envisioned and more in your life before you know it.

Alright, Bro - we coming to a close - so I am about to leave you with a few little tidbits and then it is on you to do with this, what I hope you will. Remember, when you know better, you do better. After reading this book you will know better, so you will not have any more excuses, you will know better. I am not saying that this book is the end all, be all. However, I am saying that your perspective has been changed by the words within it. It is impossible for you to have gotten to this part of the book and still look at life the same way that you did before. This book did one of two things, 1) Confirmed what you felt was right but did not know how to say it. 2) Made you completely rethink the way you looked at life. If it did more than that hit me up at rejectingthenarrative@gmail.com and tell me what else this book did for you.

Alright, so here are my last few tidbits, The Greek philosopher Socrates is given credit for the saying - "*The Unexamined Life Is Not Worth Living*" - this means that we must check ourselves and our thinking as we go throughout life. I started this book in the beginning discussing the persona that we create to handle the situations we face in life. I never said that anything was wrong with creating this persona. There will be many times you are going to need him. But like Socrates said in his quote, if we are not examining, what it is that we are doing, then it is not worth it. Whoever, your persona is, make sure that he represents you in a way that you will never have to look back on and be ashamed of. More importantly, make sure that he never does something that you will have to pay for in the end. Don't let your persona or ego, get you kicked outta school, fired from a job or have you sitting in jail. If you go back to Chapter 7, Thomas is sitting in jail for what TB decided to do… Hopefully, one day your persona and you will be one and the same.

Next, YOU MUST CREATE A SYSTEM!!! The world works on systems and routines. Success is a systematic process. Think for a second about a seed. If I put a seed on a desk will it grow? NO. Why not, because it is not in the right environment. Now, what if I take that same exact seed and put it in the ground what will happen? It will grow! Well ask yourself what is the difference? How does the seed know not to grow when it is on the desk? Why does it start to grow when it is in the dirt? Believe it or not, the seed recognizes that it is in a system in the ground and begins to work its way toward the Sun.

Without a system for success, you are as good as that seed on that desk. You are full of potential and able to do great things and produce and endless amount of fruit. You will only reach your maximum potential when you develop a system. Until then, you will remain a seed never to grow or produce fruit. However, when you are in a system you will grow endlessly and produce time and time again. Everything in nature is based on a system. The Sun rises in the morning and sets in the evening. The Birds fly south in Winter and return North in the Spring. Get in a habit of doing things repeatedly that will create a positive result.

Love them or hate them, Bill Belicheck, Greg Popovich, Nick Saban and LeBron James have their own systems that they have developed and every year you can count on them being a contender for a championship. Success is a systematic process and you must create a system in order for you to enjoy and sustain excellence.

Last thing, this is directly to my son Hannibal, but the message rings true for everyone who reads this. NOTHING IS GREATER THAN YOU… YOU ARE DIVINE… Hannibal means God's Grace - for you and every reader, you will always have God's Grace and his mercy! Both God and I want you to live right and to do right by people. Treat others with respect, dignity and honor. Life is a very precious thing that you must never take for granted and the greatest thing in life is LOVE. You have been designed with love and you come from love… No matter where you find yourself in this world, you will always have love surrounding you, it may not look like it nor feel like it. You must follow the path of love and it will always end in the reward of happiness and freedom. Hannibal, whatever you put your mind to doing, I want you know that you can achieve that and beyond.

One day, I was driving to work when I lived in Mississippi and a van cut me off and the license plate on it read I COR 2:9. I knew it was a Bible verse. 1st Corinthians Book 2 Verse 9, when I looked it up it read a message I want all of you to keep forever… "*Eyes have not seen, Ears have not heard, Nor has the mind conceived, What God has in store for those who love him.*"

Loving yourself, is loving God. You were made in his image. Loving yourself is loving other people, they are God, they were made in his image. Forever treat them with love. My son, **Flip The Scripts**. Write Your Own Destiny. Don't let the world tell you what you can and can not do, they will never see what you do because they don't have your eyes. Your vision is unique, just like Justin's in Chapter 3. You see the world differently and that is Ok, embrace it. Your will is strong, you have the strength of Kalief Browder, use it, his will and strength shutdown the Notorious jail at Riker's Island in New York. It only takes a mustard seed to move a mountain, that is God's way of telling you it only takes a little faith to do something extremely big.

Dr. Martin Luther King Jr. said that, "Procrastination is the Greatest Thief of Time!" Look fellas, tomorrow is not promised so you have to get started today. In Afeni Shakur's book Evolution of A Revolutionary, I read that, "*Pain is inevitable (you can't escape it) Suffering is optional.*" That simply means that you will not go through life without experiencing heartache - pain. However, it is a choice that we make in regards to how long we allow that pain to bother us - suffering.

I guarantee you this, you are going to suffer forever if you don't pursue your dreams but you will only feel pain during the pursuit of your dreams. If you don't give up on your pursuit, no matter how hard it gets, or how long it takes, you will one day enjoy all the pleasure that comes with success. This will only happen if you decide to **FLIP THE SCRIPTS!!!**

With Love,

Alan Gaines

Appendix I: For The Parents

Tons of depression, violence, anger and resentment in adults from the ages of 18 - 40, in my opinion, comes from not having developed the coping skills and the general know how to express their frustrations with life in a positive format. These emotions play out in a multitude of ways that often have a detrimental effect on not only their lives, but the lives of many people who they consider loved ones. In my 10 years of teaching I have seen countless parents berating children and tearing them down mentally and emotionally. Usually the adult FEELS powerless and can not afford to direct their anger and frustrations on the source of the problem. Which is usually associated with the job they hate or their current financial state. Their children often become the proverbial punching bag for the parent. Not long afterwards, primarily in their teenage years, the child has outgrown their stature and the relationship becomes contentious and strained which leads to the child losing their way.

I know you have heard this story so what is so different? Why am I telling you something that you already know? I am telling you this because as a parent and to a parent, what I plan to give your child is the gift of rejection. I am asking both of you to reject societies plan and embrace your baby as they find their path in this world. Support them despite what you think you know, because when as parents are willing to listen to our children we learn more than we could ever imagine.

I want to thank you for investing in your child in the form of buying this book. This book I assure you will stretch them and challenge them to not only think outside of the box but to give the best to themselves and also the world. - Thank You and You Are Appreciated.

Appendix II: For The Young Men

    I hope that this book allows you to find the strength of Kalief Browder. Amidst arguably, the most stressful and dire situation that a teen in America could face, Kalief Browder exemplified the most compelling Rejection Of The Narrative, I have ever heard of outside of Jesus Christ. Browder rejected the comforts and security of running with a gang that he was admittedly a member of prior to going to Riker's Island. This led to unspeakable acts of physical violence being done to him. This was only topped off by the unimaginable psychological damage he endured because he refused to plead guilty to a crime he didn't commit. Between abuse from guards and hundreds of days in solitary confinement, Browder did not break, he maintained his innocence. Browder spoke out against the injustices of Rikers and now the notorious jail is being systematically closed.

    Browder's story has enough intrigue and I strongly urge you to read and watch things about his phenomenal courage. I bring Browder up as an example, of what I believe lives within every young Black Man. The strength and courage to change the world. I strongly believe that we all hold within us the strength and courage of our convictions to not only do what is right, but to commit to ourselves, what it takes to become who we were intended to be. In order for us to accomplish these goals, we must reject the comfort and security of social acceptance, in exchange for the loneliness of sacrifice and hard work, which will pay dividends in the future.

    Making this sacrifice and commitment to ourselves, is extremely difficult for young men. Especially when your life experiences have been limited to very few places beyond the community you live in. When you compound that with the dismay of most if not all inner cities in America, I totally understand why so many of our young men take what life has given you and play the role of something you are not. You are attempting to find the momentary peace and comfort of social acceptance. Simply, you can not "see" and lack the "vision" to even want more for yourself than you already have.

    The desire for more and millions lies in all of us, but with no blueprint and an environment infested with DISCOURAGEMENT, you find yourself doing the most detrimental thing of all….SETTLING. Young brother, don't SETTLE. DO NOT CONVINCE YOURSELF THAT THIS IS ENOUGH. You were made for more and being that you were made in God's image, nothing is greater than you!

Acknowledgements

It is honestly too many people to acknowledge but I will try my best.
To My Mother - Vickie Barnes - Stansil - Thank you for all the Love and Honesty that allows me to embrace the world and others with the same love and compassion that you gave me every day of my life! I Love You Ma!

To My 2 Brothers Sherray and EJ - I am eternally grateful for everything you all have done for me - The BEST Brothers In The World. I Love Y'all

To My 2 Sisters Shellerray and BJ - It is your essence and strength that has empowered me to share my story. You both embrace the world and shine your light and seeing that makes it easy to shine mines as well! I love y'all

To Tatyana, Jaloni, Jalen, Xavier, Jalayia, Jaleah, Bryson and Demikio Jr. My Nieces and Nephews. Life and Love are awaiting you. Let the jewels that you have been handed guide your path of light - Keep Christ and his word with you at all times...

To The MEN Who Molded Me… Rodney Williams, DelRoy Bridgeman, James Welch, Charles Williams, Jeff Williams, Richard Ligon, Richard Woods, Tony Woods, Mike Woods, Ricky Haskins, Jay Johnson, Darrell Bodie, Geronimo, Larry Banks Sr. and James Piggee - Your Lessons are the Essence of This Book

To The Men Who Exposed Me To What It means to be Professional… Reginald Harrion, Chokwe Lumumba, Steve Smith, Earl Sanders and Paul Scott - Thanks for Being Mentors and the Proffessional Swag

To My A.W.D.I.P. Brothers - Bradford, Rodney, Clinton, David, Aaron, Ahkeenan, Kwaume, JJ, Paul, Jock, J Dub -& Ford & Quentin We Shared Many Narratives And Without Y'all I wouldn't have had the experiences and wisdom I shared in this book!

To the Big Homies that looked out for me when I was younger, Chaz, Rashad, Cleam, Velt, JT & Ant. Y'all showed me love and never looked down on me.

To Caleb, Calvin, Joel, Cassio & Mike Cherry - Thanks for keeping me grounded as I experienced the Turbulent 20's.

To Jeremiah, Andre, Lonnie, Sharod, Tavion, Johntrel, Britt, Curtis, Mykel, Geno, Josigha, Joseph, Bowie, DJ, Izaiah, Louis, Damon, Renfro, Bryce, Torres, Dre Javon - All The Boys at Lighthouse - Kyshawn, Tyren, Jeremy - Thanks for allowing me to be a positive influence in your life. You all inspire me just as much as you all look up to me.

To DeAndre, Kadafi, Tavares, Antoine, Adonis, Cleshawn, Emerson, Kenny, Carson, DeVante, August, Marcus, Marquise, Darion, KeVontay, Desmond, Lionnel & Koby- the best is yet to come! You all have helped me and you never knew it! Thanks

To Lacist, Amber, Tyronda, Ahronnai, Takeia, Jalissa, Ashanti, Ashanie, Jazlyn, Trin, Ophelia, Kenisha, Tierra, Devan, Shakira, Deja, Tyra - Thanks for making me a better teacher!

To Every Student and Player that I ever Taught or Coached, thank you for making me a better person and professional. Please know that every decision that I made was for your best interest. I know that I may have made mistakes, but I only wanted what was best for you! You have the power to control your destiny and know that it is never too late to make your next move your best move!

To All Readers... Always Have Wisdom & Knowledge

The Man Who Gave Me The Jewels.... Ernest Stansil Sr. & Me. Can't Put You In Words So Just Know that Hannibal Will Get the Gems You Gave Me. Love You!!!

About The Author

Alan Gaines is a happily married father of 4 beautiful children. Alan grew up in Gary, Indiana graduating from William A. Wirt High School in 2001. After graduating, Alan began college at Jackson State University in Jackson, MS. Alan would eventually transfer to Tougaloo College in Jackson, MS where he served as Mr. Tougaloo College and graduated with Honors in 2006.

In 2008, Alan returned to his hometown of Gary, Indiana where he began teaching and coaching both basketball and football. Alan began mentoring both students and players and takes pride in helping the youth he has become involved with beyond the classroom and playing fields. Alan feels that once you enter someone's life in the form of an authority figure, that is a commitment that is lifelong. So he readily extends himself towards helping them whenever possible.

Alan has made no apologies about being born to a 19 year old mother of 3. Alan's mother Vickie instilled in him to be proud of the truth. Alan's upbringing and navigation in the world has led him to give you the tools he supplied within this book. Alan loves coaching football and reading.

In 2014, Alan and his family moved to Inglewood, CA where they currently reside. Alan has transitioned from a teacher into a full time writer and public speaker.

Vickie's Kids!!! Back Row (L to R) EJ, Me, Sherray. Front Row, Shelley, Vickie and BJ

Some of my AWDIP Brothers... We Shared Plenty of Narratives...

My Wife and I on our wedding day.

My 4 Children... Anayah (top), Nehanda (bottom left) Assata holding Hannibal. Daddy loves you all... #whyIdoIt

For Booking Information Log On To:

http://www.flippingthescripts.com

Follow Me On Social Media:

Instagram: @rejectthenarrative

Twitter: @narrativereject

Facebook: flippingthescripts

Email Me At: rejectingthenarrative@gmail.com

www.ingramcontent.com/pod-product-compliance
Lightning Source LLC
Chambersburg PA
CBHW072043290426
44110CB00014B/1560